The NEW AGREEMENTS *in* Healthcare

healing a healthcare system on life support

What People Are Saying about Healthcare in America

When we have faced these so-called crises in healthcare before—health-care cost spikes, an increase in the uninsured—there was always a sense that there was some big solution coming. What's different now is there is no sense there is a big reform idea out there that might save us.

—Drew Altman, President, Henry J. Kaiser Family Foundation

The system is not going to fail like a volcano blowing its top off or the Golden Gate Bridge crashing into the ocean. What's going to happen here (in America) is not a 9/11. It's going to be a war of attrition where patient care falls apart one patient at a time.

—Myles Riner, MD, Marin General Hospital

System? What system? The delivery of healthcare in the USA was described to me, by Americans, during a recent visit as an economic jungle, a mix of excess and deprivation, lavish and inefficient, in crisis and more succinctly as chaotic.

—AR Harnden, MD, Wheatley Surgery, Oxfordshire, UK

While most Americans think they have the world's best health care, a key distinction must be made. American medicine—expertise, training and technologies for healing—is indeed the best in the world. But the health care system used to organize, deliver and pay for care is itself unhealthy to the core.

—Sidney Taurel, Chairman, President and Chief Executive Officer, Eli Lilly

What People Are Saying about
NEW AGREEMENTS Healthcare

Our work with David Dibble and New Agreements Healthcare is helping us to understand that systems, not people, are most often the reason for errors and inefficiency. And if we are to have our people help us solve our problems and prevent errors, we must create an environment where fear is replaced with love and growth. . . . I am convinced that we are becoming a significantly better organization, one that can serve as a model for what healthcare can be and what organizations can become.

—John Rossfeld, CEO, Gila Regional Medical Center

The New Agreements creates a framework for a holistic approach to the operations of an organization. We all know intuitively that it is a combination of the people and the systems that effect how well an organization operates. The New Agreements embrace the development of the people while setting them up to be successful through optimization of the systems in which they must work.

—Sue Nieboer, RN, MPA, VP Operations, Gerber Memorial Health Systems

Implementation of the New Agreements over the past 18 months has greatly improved our organization through expediting change, growing people and improving systems. . . . My clinical nursing departments are walking away from the darkness of despair and frustration and into the sunrise of happiness in the workplace.

—Cathy Woodard, CNO, Gila Regional Medical Center

I have new tools to address the need for change in the healthcare system. . . . This results in happy, productive workers and rapid change in systems and processes. I feel I'm now prepared to live my life purpose and make a real difference in the world.

—Jan Stone, MS, RN, Clinical Director, Gerber Memorial Health Systems

The NEW AGREEMENTS *in* Healthcare

healing a healthcare system on life support

DAVID DIBBLE

New Agreements Inc.
Rancho Santa Fe, California

The NEW AGREEMENTS
in Healthcare
Healing a Healthcare System on Life Support
Copyright © 2006 by David Boyd Dibble

Published by New Agreements, Inc.

P.O. Box 2674

Rancho Santa Fe, CA 92067

760-431-7893

Printed in U.S.A.

Edited by Coleen Rehm

Cover and text design by Lois Stanfield

Cover photo by John Foxx

ISBN-13 978-0-9789374-0-9   ISBN-10 0-9789374-0-6

To the Healing Human Spirit

the Essence that lives in each of us and every healthcare organization,
the Essence that co-creates with us our higher purpose,
the Essence that fills our hearts with love and compassion
the Essence that brings us home

The NEW AGREEMENTS *in* Healthcare

*healing a healthcare
system on life support*

CONTENTS

ACKNOWLEDGEMENTS

THE JOURNEY, WHICH BROUGHT US TO THIS POINT IN OUR EVOLUTION and became this book, would not have been possible without the contributions of the wonderful kindred spirits who have "showed up" to grace my life. I'd like to acknowledge the following people.

Don Miguel Ruiz, for your wisdom, friendship and unconditional love. When I think of you I can't get the smile off my face. There are few true teachers walking the earth. You are one. It was an honor to be your student and I consider you my best friend. Time and distance have no affect on the love Linda and I have for you.

John Rossfeld, for your courage in giving me and the New Agreements a chance to prove that we really could make a sustainable difference in healthcare. This book and the good work we did at Gila Regional Medical Center would not have been possible without you.

My dad, the fisherman, for demonstrating the healing power of the whole—body, mind and spirit.

Mom, Lola, and Bob for your love and support and for being part of this ongoing saga of healthcare in America.

Attendees of New Agreements Healthcare Teacher Training: You are the pioneers who have proven that it's possible to evolve from student to teacher at warp speed. Healthcare needs you. It's been my honor to work with you in this way.

Christine Ho and Sara Gilman, the first Graduate Mentors of New Agreements Healthcare Teacher Training. Your commitment to this work and your personal and professional growth is remarkable. I'm honored to work with you in this way.

Lois Stanfield, for your beautiful cover and interior design of this book. You visually captured the essence of the message and this work. Coleen Rehm, for your superb editorial work and commitment to making a difference in this world. You kept me on track in our mad dash to publication.

Gratitude for our incredible children and teachers, Steve, Mike, and Quinn. There is no operations manual that magically appears when babies come into the world. So, like all flawed and ill-equipped parents, we did our best to guide you to become happy, productive adults. You're all that and more. You are fully connected to your humanity. We feel so blessed to have you in our lives.

Linda, my wife of thirty-five years—confidant, lover and friend. It's difficult to believe that it's taken us almost six decades to learn enough to begin this work. You're my Italian beauty that keeps me on the planet and reminds me to put the cap on the toothpaste.

And finally, I want to acknowledge *you*, the new leaders who will be on the frontlines in the coming transformation of healthcare in America. I look forward to this magnificent and purposeful journey with you. Thank you, thank you, thank you.

—*David Dibble*

INTRODUCTION

The greatest mistake in the treatment of diseases is that there are physicians for the body and physicians for the soul, although the two cannot be separated.

—Plato

A Call for Help

THE HEALTHCARE SYSTEM IN THIS COUNTRY IS IN DIRE NEED OF resuscitation. Yet, when the question of what needs to be fixed about healthcare is thoroughly examined, we find that it's largely a matter of simply acknowledging and addressing basic systems problems. In fact, these types of systems issues are so prevalent that it's more the norm than the exception in our hospitals today.

An accomplished physician in his field who works for one of the top 15 hospitals in the nation received the following letter from an OR nurse. He read it during a New Agreements Teacher Training to illustrate the current healthcare situation. What you're about to read is typical of the scope of systems problems that currently plague healthcare facilities. Names and other identifying information have been changed to protect the privacy of the innocent individuals involved.

The physician who read this letter couldn't get all the way through it without stopping to shed a tear or two. I seldom have to go for the tissue box at these trainings, but I, too, was moved by this letter. We all were. A piece of each of us resides in the heart of this caregiver who related her typical day in the operating room (OR) in 2006.

A Nursing Account of a Typical OR Day

This is not a litany of complaints. This is not one OR person "blaming" others. This is merely a commentary on one case that unfortunately is very representative of what we are doing in every single case.

Room 9, a relatively simple Dr. "X" spine procedure at 0730 on Tuesday.

We did not have a 6:00 A.M. person setting up our rooms. The room did have a Jackson table with a Wilson frame on it. There were no dressings for the Wilson frame, and no face pillow. There was no "crank" for the Wilson, and the only one in the drawer in Room 10 was the wrong one.

Our float person was covering another room until 8:00 A.M.

The regular computer was not working. I had phoned the help desk two weeks earlier about the problem; it was never fixed. Today it was a problem because our films were from an outside hospital and they were on a disc. Three phone calls to the help desk eventually brought a technician to the room. NIC notified.

Case was not booked with a C-arm. Dr. "Y" notified the office of Dr. "X" about the importance of doing this. Two phone calls to X-ray. The radiology tech was very gracious and did manage to secure a C-arm for an hour or so.

No microscope in Room 9. We claimed one that "J" and "B" were with (labeled Room 11) and eventually were able to locate the matching monitor, which was not in our area.

Two individual lights in the OR lights were out. Called Bio Med.

The spine set for Dr. "X" contained two rongeurs that were caked with old bone. I bagged and tagged them, notified the NIC, she notified "K" from Quality Control and I ordered a Laminectomy I and II from Central Processing. I visited clean holding twice to collect them. The needed instruments in that kit were also dirty.

"K" came asking for the "slips" from the offending kits.

My room had one step stool. I borrowed another from Room 10, which was very soiled with blood and bone. I borrowed another. The care assistants did clean up the first one.

The arm board attached to the Jackson table broke as the anesthesia attending slid it higher on the table. The patient's arm did not fall. I located a care assistant who was dispatched to find another arm board.

My room (cabinets) were poorly stocked and in disarray. There were three incomplete Neuro prep kits, no body part for the hairclipper, no one-inch paper tape, no gelfoam, and 15 boxes of random sutures on the shelves though the Neuro sutures were depleted. I had one ring stand only and a broken lid on one of the trash containers. At noon there were no towels on the exchange cart, nor were there any 60cc syringes, or 1000 drapes. Those were just the items I went looking for.

When my case finished, I took the patient to the recovery room, went to pre-op to see the next patient and returned to the OR to start setting up. I was not able to clear the old sutures out of the cabinet or gather supplies to re-stock the rooms. I did ask the supply room to come and make a list, but I never saw that happen. My apologies to the person who relieved me at three o'clock. . . . and I guess that's where we're at . . . it's a mess . . . I'm sorry, but it just isn't getting done . . . run in and out of the adjoining rooms, scramble for what you need, borrow one of these and lend something in return.

I know you can read between the lines. Every one of these simple items represents distractions, hurriedness, one more phone call, more waiting, time out of the OR and time away from surgery.

Help!

Similar scenarios play out day after day in hospitals across the nation and it is not only in the operating room. It also shows up in various departments throughout healthcare organizations. In many ways, the healthcare delivery system in America is simply broken. The only thing holding it loosely together is the energy, commitment and dedication of caregivers who are forced to work in these dysfunctional systems.

Healthcare in America can be fixed, but not by doing the same things over and over while expecting a different result.

In virtually all cases, statistical thinking equaled
or surpassed human judgment.
—Atul Gawande, MD, Assistant Professor, Health Policy and Management,
Harvard School of Public Health
Complications: A Surgeon's Notes on an Imperfect Science

Systems Theory and Universal Principles

SYSTEMS THEORY AND UNIVERSAL PRINCIPLES SHOW US THAT AT LEAST 90 percent of the results we experience in healthcare are a function of the systems in which healthcare is delivered. One focus of this book is the real-world story of what it will take to fix our healthcare systems. Another focus is transformation: the growth and change that occurs in people (the leaders, caregivers and patients) who are most affected by the current healthcare system. And third, it is about a new possibility for American healthcare that moves beyond curing to the holistic arena of healing and wellness.

Healing and wellness go beyond the physical body. They go beyond the mechanical, impersonal methodologies that have infected many of our healthcare organizations. We have to begin to see patients and each other as whole beings: body, mind and spirit. Additionally, we must begin to recognize the healing power of human compassion—and *love*.

Getting from Here to There

FOR MORE THAN TWO DECADES, I JOURNEYED ON A PATH OF self-understanding. It was a spiritual journey that took me into the essence of a number of ancient bodies of knowledge including Christianity, Hinduism, Buddhism, Native American teachings, Toltec wisdom, Siddha Yoga, and more. I found that, at their essence, the teachings of these and other great bodies of knowledge were the same. While the principles were stated in different ways, they were nevertheless universal. Most importantly, these principles applied to the workplace as much as our personal lives.

In 2002, I wrote *The New Agreements in the Workplace: Releasing the Human Spirit*. Although the book did not become the runaway best seller as I had optimistically predicted, I knew that the information shared in the book was useful and possibly even profound. The New Agreements are a roadmap for transforming the workplace from a place of fear and control to a place of love, joy, support and quality. More importantly, these systems-based implementation strategies produce *significant increases to the bottom line.*

The New Agreements comprise the powerful combination of Systems Thinking, Best Business Practices, Universal/Spiritual Principles, and the wisdom of some of the greatest thinkers who have graced our planet. Still I knew that unless there was a way to apply these bodies of knowledge in a practical way to the real world of business, organization and leadership, there would be little general acceptance of New Agreements methodologies as a catalyst for organizational change.

I needed a guinea pig. I needed a company that would implement the New Agreements to prove that they were indeed a roadmap for organizational change. So I set out to find a company that was willing to apply New Agreements principles and measure the results.

For almost three years I searched for the company that would be willing to be the first New Agreements model. No good candidates showed up. After a number of disappointments, I surrendered to the fact that I didn't run the universe and that if it was meant to be, the perfect company would emerge.

Of course shortly after my unconditional surrender, I received a call out of the blue from Gila Regional Medical Center, a hospital of 650 caregivers in picturesque Silver City, New Mexico.

"Where in the heck is Silver City?" I asked Brian Cunningham, Director of Gila Regional Wellness Center.

"It's easy to find," he assured me. "Fly to Tucson. Rent a car. Drive east for a couple of hours, turn left and drive for another hour. Simple.

You can't miss it. As a matter of fact, the only way to get to Silver City is to go to Silver City. It's not on the way to anywhere else." We enjoyed a hearty laugh together.

In a conference call with Gila Regional CEO John Rossfeld, I was asked if I had ever worked with a hospital previously in my business consulting. I said no.

He asked if I knew anything about healthcare. I said that I knew it wasn't working very well, but no, I didn't know anything about healthcare. He asked why they should hire someone who knew nothing about their business or industry to help them change and improve.

In a moment of honesty (or highly refined stupidity) I replied that I didn't have a logical, plausible business argument for hiring us. However, I did have faith that hiring us was the right thing to do. I shared with John that the hospital should hire us because Gila Regional was *the* organization that was to become the first New Agreements model for the transformation of healthcare in America.

"How do you know that?" John asked.

In another leap of faith, I shared that Gila Regional had been shown to me in meditation as the New Agreements model two days prior to our current conference call. I told him, without a doubt, "You're the one." The laughter we shared was genuine.

I added that maybe *not* knowing about the industry was an asset instead of a liability. I reminded him of a quote from Mark Twain: "It ain't what you don't know that gets you into trouble. It's what you know for sure, that just ain't so."

I didn't have blind spots and so was free to ask the most inane and ignorant questions. Besides, the New Agreements principles were universal and would work in almost any business or workplace environment. They would certainly work in healthcare—or so I believed. I suggested a one-day visit to the hospital so people could "kick the tires" and learn a little more about the New Agreements and how we might apply them at Gila Regional.

I flew to Tucson, rented a car, drove east for two hours, turned left, drove for another hour, and presto! I was in Silver City. I met with all the key players and decision makers and enjoyed myself immensely. People were engaged, interested, honest, curious, thoughtful and, for the most part, clear that something must change at Gila Regional if they were to progress and improve in today's challenging healthcare environment. One week after my visit, Gila Regional made the decision to move forward and work with me and the New Agreements model. We all knew that moving forward meant going beyond traditional healthcare mindsets and culture. And so the adventure began. From it sprang the inception of this book.

The New Agreements in Healthcare considers great possibilities for healthcare in America. While the context of this real-world tale is applying the universal principles embodied in the New Agreements as a new model for healthcare in America, it is also about you.

It is about people—their growth, inspiration, commitment and perspiration that ultimately recreates their lives, both professionally and personally. As you read this book, look for yourself in its pages. Parts of what you read will resonate deeply within you. There may be times when you feel inspired or called to action in some way. To the best of your ability, look for those things that call to you.

In Chapter 1 ("American Healthcare: A System on Life Support") we will look at the current critical condition of healthcare in America. One universal systems principle is that we generally should not attempt to solve a problem until the problem is understood. Good or not-so-good, it is best to start as close to the truth as possible, even if that truth is uncomfortable.

Chapter 2 shows how dysfunction in the American healthcare system is draining the life energy out of the people who most need a working healthcare system—patients and caregivers.

Chapter 3 introduces my friend and former teacher, don Miguel Ruiz and his wonderful Four Agreements. The Four Agreements are a foundational building block for creating a new way of operating and being in healthcare. As Miguel says so well, practicing the Four Agreements is "a way to gain your personal freedom."

Chapter 4 presents New Agreements Healthcare. The New Agreements are a now-proven roadmap for transforming healthcare in America. The New Agreements, in conjunction with the Four Agreements, offer a holistic, workable model for organizational, professional and personal change in healthcare.

Chapter 5 introduces Planetree, a philosophy and working model for patient-centered care that addresses the whole human being: body, mind, spirit. In addition, we are treated to an understanding of how the power of healing environments enhances patient recoveries.

Chapter 6 ("New Agreements Healthcare in Action") moves us from good ideas and intentions to action. This chapter describes the measurable results of real-world implementation of New Agreements

Healthcare at Gila Regional Medical Center and presents the financial benefit to the bottom line.

The New Agreements Healthcare Teacher Training is the focus for Chapter 7. Without strong internal support systems, including champions and teachers proficient at teaching and modeling New Agreements Healthcare attitudes and skills, its sustainability in a healthcare organization would be thrown into question. See how the Teacher Training creates outside consultants and teachers, as well as internal leaders and champions, while dramatically transforming the lives of participants, both professionally and personally.

As in any great adventure, much learning comes our way. In Chapter 8, we examine the lessons learned at Gila Regional Medical Center in the first ever implementation of New Agreements Healthcare in an American healthcare organization. Some lessons we learned were predictable, although there were some real surprises, too.

Finally Chapter 9 outlines future possibilities for healthcare based on wellness. We see how caregivers must lead the change they wish to see in healthcare and the world.

Every time I think I might have accomplished something or evolved to a higher understanding of life, all I have to do is look back to the evolved being I thought I was only a short time ago. In 2002, when I wrote my first book, *The New Agreements in the Workplace*, I was sure that the book contained meaningful insights, etched in stone that would benefit the workplace and life in general. Of course, it turns out that in four short years much has evolved and changed—including me.

The universal principles of 2002 or 2006 or even 200,006 are still eternal. It is in the mind where most human evolution takes place. *The New Agreements in Healthcare* has, in some ways, moved beyond *The New Agreements in the Workplace*. The Agreements themselves have changed in subtle yet powerful ways. Four years from today the Agreements may change again. But for today, the journey you are about to embark upon with me is from our most evolved point in the human experience at this point in time. I believe you will discover an authentic part of yourself resonating within these pages. Welcome to *The New Agreements in Healthcare: Healing a Healthcare System on Life Support.*

AMERICAN HEALTHCARE:
A SYSTEM ON LIFE SUPPORT

I firmly believe that if the whole materia medica *could be sunk to the bottom of the sea, it would be all the better for mankind and all the worse for the fishes.*

—Oliver Wendell Holmes

IN AMERICA, WE ARE EVOLVING INTO A NATION OF SICK PEOPLE. The great majority of illnesses, which clog our hospitals, emergency rooms and drug stores are now self-inflicted from the way that we live our lives. We, the people, are becoming chronically sick in larger numbers. In the process, the "healthcare" system in America has become a "sick-care" system. With health out the window in favor of tending to the ever-increasing number of sick Americans, healthcare itself has also become sick. As in all conditions of dis-ease, there is a body-mind-spirit connection. Healthcare, which focuses on problems in the body, finds itself with a mindset and lack of higher purpose that practically guarantees that it will continue to slip even deeper into its sad malaise.

Much of our current healthcare is about curing. Curing is good.
But healing is spiritual, and healing is better, because we can heal
many people we cannot cure.
—Susan Frampton, Laura Gilpin and Patrick Charmel
Putting Patients First: Designing and Practicing Patient-Centered Care

Healthcare in America, as we know it, appears to be careening toward a terminal condition. The source of the disease is a slow and invisible killer that only exhibits its full potential for dysfunction toward the end of the life cycle. The pathogens that are making healthcare so sick are the legacy healthcare systems, in which we are forced to deliver care. Like all systems that resist change in a changing environment, they become more complex and dysfunctional by the day.

It is a universal principle that systems that resist change in a changing environment require more and more energy to maintain the status quo. That energy has to come from somewhere. Much of it comes from the people who seek medical help (patients) and those who are forced to work in these increasingly complex and inefficient systems (caregivers). For the most part, it is the caregivers who use more and more of their energy to hold the crumbling healthcare systems together.

However caregivers are running low on energy, resulting in burnout and mistakes that produce accelerating numbers of people leaving healthcare as fewer people are drawn into the profession. This is a ship heading for an iceberg while the captain loudly calls his usual orders to the boiler room, "More energy! Full speed ahead!"

In addition, customers of American healthcare—patients—also pay a big price. The quality of the care they receive continues to decline as the cost of that care continues to rise.

Wherever costs are passed on through employers and other pay-ers, energy flows from more productive parts of society to an increasingly inefficient "sick-care" system, weakening the whole. American healthcare has become so expensive that the vast majority of Americans cannot afford to spend even a moderate amount of time in the hospital, whether they are covered by insurance or not.

Nearly forty-six million Americans are currently uninsured. Tens of millions more are underinsured and would be financially ruined by any medical problem that required extended hospitalization.

It is no secret that the healthcare system in America has many problems. Yet many Americans, including the vested interests and a majority of our political leaders, are in denial about the current condition of healthcare in America. Data indicates that problems are so severe and systems so dysfunctional that healthcare in America is comparable to a dinosaur waiting for the weather to change. And the weather *is* changing. A hurricane of change is rapidly churning its way toward an ill-prepared American healthcare system.

National demographics and lifestyles are working overtime against an American healthcare system already on life support. The number of people who will require hospitalization continues to rise as we, as a nation, grow heavier, older and chronically sicker. For example, soon more than 80 million sick and aging Baby Boomers will be flooding our emergency rooms and hospitals. Who will pay for this increased burden? And the captain's shrill command still remains the same, "More energy! Full speed ahead!"

Without being disrespectful, I consider the U.S. healthcare delivery system the largest cottage industry in the world. There are virtually no performance measurements and no standards. Trying to measure performance ... is the next revolution in healthcare.

—Richard Huber, former Aetna CEO

Donald L. Bartlett and James B. Steele, two Pulitzer Prize-winning journalists for investigative reporting, unearthed the following facts and published them in *Critical Condition: How Health Care in America Became Big Business—and Bad Medicine:*

Many countries around the world take far better care of their people, achieve better results from their health care systems, and do it all with far fewer dollars. In 2001, per capita health care spending in the United States amounted to $4,887. That was 75 percent more than the $2,792 that Canada spent. Yet Canadians can expect to live two and a half years longer than Americans. The Canadian life span at birth: 79.8 years. The American: 77.1 years. U.S. spending was 205 percent greater than Spain, yet the Spanish can expect to live 2.1 years longer. As for the Japanese, with a life span of 80.9 years, the world's longest, they can expect to live nearly four years longer than Americans. This even though Japan's per capita spending on health care is only 41 percent of US outlays. In sum, Americans pay for a Hummer but get a Ford Escort.

On this scale, the United States does not even rank in the top ten. But the statistics are even grimmer when life span is counted in years of healthy living. A comparatively new yardstick devised by the World Health Organization (WHO), this formula subtracts from traditional life expectancy the number of years spent in poor health, the years when individuals are unable to engage in all the activities their peers do, when they are confined to beds in nursing homes and must be fed by someone else. By this measure, the United States in 2002 ranked a distant 29th among the countries of the world, between Slovenia and Portugal.

Then there is the fact that the vast majority of healthcare delivery is *not* measured, *not* evaluated, *not* improved in any way, and—worst of all—*not* seen as a *delivery system*, which it is.

In order to *see* systems, one must become a *systems thinker*. Yet the great majority of people in healthcare leadership positions are not systems thinkers and so they have virtually no means with which to correct flaws in the system. Instead, we jump up and down in what becomes a never-ending parade of action-reaction drama.

> *Practice variation is not caused by* bad *or* ignorant *doctors.*
> *Rather, it is a natural consequence of a system that systematically tracks neither its processes nor its outcomes . . . For instance, when family practitioners in Washington State were queried about treating a simple urinary tract infection, 82 physicians came up with an extraordinary 137 strategies.*
>
> —Michael L. Millenson, MD, Director, Hematology Service,
> Fox Chase Cancer Center
> *Demanding Medical Excellence: Doctors and Accountability in the Information Age*

As with any system in which there is a high degree of variation, results are not predictable and costs tend to be high or even outlandish. It appears that the American healthcare system is conforming quite well to universal systems principles in its dysfunction. We can expect things to continue to deteriorate unless we make sweeping changes to the foundation of the current system. In the meantime, patients, caregivers and other constituencies suffer under the never-ending crunch of higher costs due to caregivers working longer, more stressful hours producing multiple mistakes, lower quality care and general drama. The result of all this dysfunction is that patients get marginal care at higher prices, while caregivers and physicians are worn down by the constant grind and stress of working in inefficient systems.

In the next chapter we'll explore how dysfunction in the current American healthcare system is draining the life out of patients and caregivers alike.

PATIENTS AND CAREGIVERS IN CRITICAL CONDITION

Never go to a doctor whose office plants have died.
—Erma Bombeck

I HAVE COLLECTED REAL-LIFE STORIES OF THE DYSFUNCTION IN THE present healthcare system for this book. To say that one doesn't have to look hard to find these types of stories would be a gross understatement.

Dangerous Near-Discharge

BOB CLARKE IS MY FATHER-IN-LAW. HE IS AN INCREDIBLE MAN—talented, loving and wonderfully humble. A former pilot and veteran of WW II, Bob is now 89 years old. He has seen a lot in his many years and has shared his wisdom with us in his flair for story-telling and writing. Here's Bob's story of his dangerous near-discharge.

Bob has had a number of health issues that required time in the hospital. Heart problems and liver cancer are the most troublesome. Bob has been fortunate to have very good doctors and been a patient in only highly rated hospitals. Here are a few of his experiences while having a relatively minor procedure done at one of the "best" hospitals in America.

He arrived at the hospital at the specified time for his procedure, but someone forgot to schedule him so there was no room available. He was told that they could get him in if he cared to wait an hour. Three hours later he was told to go home. No room would be available for him and the machine that they would be using for his procedure had broken down. He was asked to come back the following day.

The following day he arrived at the specified time and waited for an hour for his room. Some of the problems he encountered during his stay were the following: staff couldn't find a wheelchair to take him to his room; the room had no telephone; there were no toiletries in the bathroom, it appeared unclean and the light was burned out; and his meals were never what he ordered.

The day after the procedure, Bob was told that he was being discharged. Again no wheelchair could be found to transport him out of the hospital and he waited a full hour before the wheelchair arrived. On the way out Bob's wife, Lola, stopped one of Bob's doctors who happened to be walking by and asked if the doctor was sure Bob should be discharged so soon after the procedure. The doctor looked shocked.

"No, he can't go yet," he exclaimed. "His potassium level is too low and must be stabilized before he goes home!" Bob waited and was finally wheeled to another room and given an IV to stabilize his potassium level. We later learned that it would have been very dangerous had he left the hospital prior to having his potassium level stabilized.

More than Emotional Distress

LINDA'S AUNT MARY WENT INTO THE HOSPITAL WITH SOME SERIOUS health concerns. Luckily, she had ample health insurance and was a patient at one of the most respected hospitals in Los Angeles.

After a few days in the hospital, Mary complained that she almost never saw her doctor and the nurses seemed too busy to check in on her or follow through on her many requests and complaints. Lola, Mary's sister-in-law and caretaker, visited Mary often. Lola was shocked by the attitude and lack of attentiveness of the people at the hospital.

One night at 3:00 a.m., Lola received a call from hospital staff, informing her that Mary had died and that Lola should come to the hospital to pick up her personal effects. Shocked and beside herself with grief, Lola drove straight to the hospital in the middle of the night.

When she arrived at the hospital, she was told that the records of Mary's death could not be located. Nursing staff decided to check in Mary's room. There was Mary, sleeping peacefully in her bed. It seems another lady had died during the night and the staff received misinformation that the deceased was Mary.

In the meantime, all of Mary clothes and personal effects had been taken from her room by unidentified nursing or housekeeping staff. With little concern for the emotional distress that the hospital staff had put her through, Lola was assured that Mary's clothes and personal belongings would be found and immediately returned to her room. The clothes and other personal items, some of which were emotionally significant to Mary, were never found. However, staff told Lola that she could petition the hospital to request partial compensation for the lost items.

Oversight Results in Complications

MY MOTHER WENT INTO THE HOSPITAL TO HAVE MINOR SURGERY ON A drooping eyelid. The fact that she has a blood disorder, which slows clotting and causes her to bleed, was unfortunately overlooked in her records.

After the procedure, she was sent home with a huge bandage over one side of her face. She continued to bleed for three days with the doctor assuring her that the bleeding would soon stop on its own.

Finally the doctor instructed her to come in. After several hours they were able to stop the bleeding. Months later, the eye has not healed completely. Since the procedure, my mother's eye is now sensitive, perpetually red and waters constantly.

No day passed—not one—without a medication error. The errors were not rare; they were the norm. One medication was discontinued by a physician's order on the first day of my wife's admission and yet was brought by a nurse every single evening for 14 days straight.

— Don Berwick, MD, President, CEO, and co-founder of the Institute for Healthcare Improvement

Finally, note this report written by Jason Riley, published in *The Courier-Journal*, August 2, 2006:

A jury yesterday found University Hospital negligent in a surgery that led to the death of a Kentucky woman, and it awarded the woman's family more than $9 million.

The hospital was responsible for damages involved in the death of Brandenburg resident Jennifer Beglin, 40, who had elective surgery on July 14, 2003, and died that October, the Jefferson Circuit Court jury found.

During the surgery, Beglin suffered massive blood loss and despite more than a dozen calls to the hospital blood bank a floor below, the blood was delayed in getting to Beglin, causing her to suffer brain damage, go into a coma and eventually die, said Jack Conway, an attorney for the Beglin family.

The systems problems that caused the situation that required "more than a dozen calls to the hospital blood bank a floor below" is no different from a systems standpoint than the one that causes a wheelchair not to be available to Bob when he was leaving the hospital.

People tried their best to serve the patient, but dysfunction in systems guarantee that there will be times when blood won't make it to surgery in time to save the patient or that a wheelchair will not be available when a patient is ready to leave the hospital. Poor systems are the real cause behind all of the above described situations.

These are the facts: 90 percent of the results we experience in healthcare, both good and not-so-good, are a function of the systems in which people work—not their individual efforts. In the next twelve months, 100,000 Americans will die and two million more will be injured in healthcare with over 90 percent of this carnage due to legacy systems that remain, for the most part, *invisible* to our leaders and managers in healthcare. Because the systems are invisible to leaders who are not *systems thinkers*, the root causes of problems are never addressed. The result? We fight the same fires over and over with similar strategies and expect a different result. Perfect insanity? Undoubtedly. And the caregivers who work in these poor systems are affected, too.

No Chance for Caregivers Either

WHILE IT IS LIKELY THAT MANY OF US HAVE SIMILAR STORIES OR KNOW people who have had similar experiences in hospitals, there is an even bigger story evolving from the disenfranchised caregivers who have to work in America's dysfunctional healthcare systems.

From the outside, it appears that nurses, doctors and staff are making mistakes, are inefficient, have poor attitudes, do shoddy work, don't seem to care, don't share information, are cold or unfeeling, and just can't seem to do anything right. Nothing could be further from the truth.

For the most part, the people in healthcare went into that profession because they wanted to do something meaningful. They wanted to serve. They wanted to cure the sick and heal the injured. They wanted to make a difference.

However, caregivers working in dysfunctional systems get beaten down by those systems. Remember the call-for-help letter from the dedicated OR nurse in the Introduction? Regardless of how hard they try, the staff is only able to deliver what the system allows them to deliver. This fact is not well-known to leaders and managers in healthcare. However, known or unknown, it is still a fact that systems principles are at work in healthcare.

When over 90 percent of the results we experience in healthcare are a function of the systems in which caregivers work and *not* their individual efforts, the case for systems thinking and systems literacy—especially for leaders and managers—is a strong one. In the vast majority of cases, ignorance of systems causes leaders and managers to mistakenly blame people for systems problems.

Again, 90 percent of the results we experience in healthcare (good or not-so-good) are a function of the systems in which people work, not their individual efforts. Almost no one wakes up in the morning and thinks, *I'll go to the hospital today and make as many mistakes as possible.* A core issue in healthcare today is that leaders are not systems literate. Until we fix the systems, we're going to get what we're getting now.

Then things will get worse. If you look at healthcare in America, this is exactly what has happened in the last few decades. These universal systems principles cannot be overridden by any CEO, leader or manager, including the powers that be in our government. You might remember the famous line from the movie *Apollo 13*, "Houston, we have a problem." Here in America, we have a problem, too. We have a problem in healthcare—a systems problem.

While it is sobering to reflect on the current condition of healthcare in America, it is also a time of great potential. The first step in solving any problem is to understand it (another basic systems principle).

Then, we face the real challenge. What are we going to do about it? Is there a new model for healthcare in America to which we can aspire? The answer is *yes*. New Agreements Healthcare and Miguel Ruiz' Four Agreements appear to offer a model for transforming healthcare. In the next chapter we will examine "The Four Agreements" as they apply to healthcare.

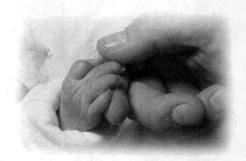

THE FOUR AGREEMENTS

The only theology worth doing is that which inspires and transforms lives, that which empowers us to participate in creating, liberating, and blessing the world.

—Carter Heyward, Ph.D., Professor of Theology, Episcopal Divinity School

DON MIGUEL RUIZ IS THE AUTHOR OF THE WORLDWIDE BEST-SELLING book, *The Four Agreements*, which has sold more than 3 million copies. Miguel was also my teacher from 1990 to 1998 from whom I learned about a path to personal freedom. I was a good student and learned as much as possible. Then in 1998, Miguel "kicked me out," telling me that it was now my time to teach.

My work and life purpose happens to be translating these universal principles so that they are easily understood in the workplace. It's also teaching organizations how to apply the principles to better their performance and increase their contributions to society. I still see Miguel socially and thoroughly enjoy our time together. He says he likes to hang around me because I make him laugh and laughter is healing.

We studied the Four Agreements long before the book was published and sought to make them real in our lives. As simple and powerful as the Four Agreements are as a guide to personal freedom, they are a challenge, too. As anyone who has attempted to live the Four Agreements might attest, it is easy to forget about the Agreements when faced with the ongoing challenge of everyday living. Still, it is more than worth the effort to practice and master the Agreements because mastering the Agreements equates to a certain level of mastery in life.

Before we go any further, let's take a minute to review don Miguel Ruiz's Four Agreements as his guide to personal freedom and explore what they might mean when applied to a healthcare setting.

The First Agreement: Be Impeccable with Your Word

Speak with integrity. Say only what you mean. Avoid using the word to speak against yourself or to gossip about others. Use the power of your word in the direction of truth and love.

—don Migues Ruiz

THE WAY IMPECCABILITY WITH YOUR WORDS MIGHT APPLY IN HEALTHCARE and the workplace in general is in the power of speaking with good purpose. The *word* is the most powerful tool in humanity's toolbox. Every word starts with a thought. Have we chosen a thought that comes with good purpose, compassion and love? We must remember to examine our thoughts and then chose the most appropriate words (tools of communication).

Before you speak, ask yourself this question: *Do these words come from love or fear?* If they come from love, they are probably going to communicate what you want to communicate. If they come from fear, you may be setting yourself up for a learning experience. In some cases, being impeccable with your word means choosing *not* to speak if that is most appropriate to the situation. Can you see how this one agreement might reduce mistakes, miscommunication, politics and gossip in the workplace? Miguel says that mastering this single agreement can create heaven on earth.

The Second Agreement: Don't Take Anything Personally

Nothing others do is because of you. What others say and do is a projection of their own reality, their own dream. When you are immune to the opinions and actions of others, you won't be the victim of needless suffering.
—don Migues Ruiz

WE MUST REALIZE THAT WHAT OTHERS SAY AND THINK ABOUT US IS NOT important, and so we can decline to take things personally. Their words, agendas and gossip have nothing to do with who we really are in the workplace. When we become unattached to what others say, think and do, we become concerned *only* with being the best we can be. This frees us to be more alive and energetic both in the workplace and at home. Remember, what others say about us says more about them than it does about us.

The Third Agreement: Don't Make Assumptions

Find the courage to ask questions and to express what you really want. Communicate with others as clearly as you can to avoid misunderstandings, sadness and drama. With just this one agreement, you can completely transform your life.

—don Migues Ruiz

MAKING ASSUMPTIONS IS ONE OF THE FASTEST WAYS TO CREATE MISCOMmunication and drama in our work lives. In most workplaces, we waste a great deal of time and energy dealing with politics, gossip and solving problems that were created because we or others made assumptions that weren't true. Take actions based upon good data whenever possible and avoid making assumptions, especially those that are fear-based.

The Fourth Agreement: Always Do Your Best

Your best is going to change from moment to moment; it will be different when you are healthy as opposed to sick. Under any circumstance, simply do your best and you will avoid self-judgment, self-abuse and regret.

—don Migues Ruiz

MOST OF US DO THE BEST WE CAN UNDER THE CIRCUMSTANCES. OUR BEST will vary from time to time, but if we know we've done our best, we can be kind to ourselves regardless of the results we create. We must remember that we can be only as kind to others as we are to ourselves. In the new healthcare system, kindness to self and others will become a way of operating.

Can you imagine everyone in your workplace being impeccable with their words? Not taking things personally? Not making assumptions? Doing their best all the time? Imagine what it would be like if everyone in all healthcare organizations behaved this way.

Incorporating the Four Agreements into healthcare is a great idea, but they must become more than an idea or concept in order to bring value to the workplace. We must *become* the Four Agreements. We must begin by practicing what we desire to become: We must become living role models and conduct our lives in ways that embody the Four Agreements.

For those of you who are already using the Four Agreements as a guideline for improving your lives, you probably know how easy it is to forget to *live* the agreements. That's because the changes you're attempting to make are changes in your mind. Most of the time, our minds run freely, spinning out thoughts, beliefs and memories, without us being a conscious part of the process. The fears in our minds often create realities that are less than desirable, while we merely go along for the ride.

How then do we begin to gain control of our minds so that we can have some control over what we experience in our lives? This is where the Masteries come into play.

The Masteries

THERE ARE THREE AREAS OF LIFE THAT MUST BE MASTERED: AWARENESS, Transformation and Intent. When one becomes a master of Awareness, Transformation and Intent, one masters life. A master of life creates the life he or she desires, both at work and at home.

The Mastery of Awareness

THE FIRST MASTERY INVOLVES WAKING UP TO THE FACT THAT YOU ARE not your mind. It means knowing that you are much more than what you think, believe and remember. Without the Mastery of Awareness, virtually nothing is possible; your mind just runs on automatic pilot and you receive whatever comes along in life.

Yet with heightened awareness, you can begin to work toward making your mind your ally. You can use your mind as a powerful, wonderful tool to enhance your life and the lives of others.

The purpose of your mind is to create your reality. Your mind is made up of your thoughts, beliefs and memories. Your mind is that little voice in your head that constantly comments on everything you are and everything you do.

I'll ask your forgiveness in advance for my candor with this next comment. The best description I have heard of this little voice that constantly talks and criticizes everything is "the itty-bitty-shitty committee." When you're listening to your thoughts, you're listening to your mind. It's that little voice that may be saying, "What little voice?" or "Oh yeah, I know that 'committee' well."

Being aware of what your mind thinks, believes and remembers gives you the chance to change your reality. As it is on the inside, so it is on the outside. In other words, everything happens inside out. To change your world, you must first change your mind. That's because your mind creates your reality or world. If we're talking about changing healthcare, we're talking about changing the mind-set or culture of healthcare organizations. In either case, change starts with awareness and it begins within.

Two types of awareness are critical in transforming healthcare organizations. The first is an awareness of what your individual mind is doing. The second is an awareness of the systems that create dysfunction in the workplace. Systems literacy (described in more detail later in this book) is crucial if you are going to achieve a mastery of awareness in your life and in the workplace.

The Mastery of Awareness is the cornerstone for the other Masteries. Nothing meaningful can be accomplished in the area of either personal transformation or transformation of the workplace without first having some degree of awareness. Without awareness, the Four Agreements become nothing more than a nice concept instead of a practical guide to creating a more supportive workplace.

Practicing the Mastery of Awareness requires the following three simple steps:

(1) Catch yourself in the moment

(2) Observe what's going on—inside and out

(3) Make a choice

Step I: Catch Yourself in the Moment

THE THREE STEPS CAN BE EASILY EXPLAINED BY APPLYING THEM TO AN example. Let's say you frequently behave in an impatient or frustrated manner when you can't find a wheelchair for your patient. You don't like how this makes you feel and you want to change your habitual reaction to this situation. The first step is to start catching yourself at the moment you start feeling frustrated or behaving impatiently. Most people are pretty good at catching themselves after the fact, but looking back is an almost meaningless activity. You must catch yourself in the moment.

The key to changing is not to try to change, but first to become aware of what's happening in real-time.

As a human being with little awareness, almost everything you do is done automatically. You probably don't say to yourself, *I think I'll be really frustrated because I can't find a wheelchair* or *I think I'll get angry at housekeeping for not cleaning this room.* You just feel frustrated or get angry when circumstances or something in the environment triggers that type of emotion in you. The mind is running the show and you are being dragged along for the ride. It's the action-reaction life that most of us experience as "normal."

If you do not become aware of your thoughts (and the emotions or feelings that are part of those thoughts), you have no chance of creating proactive change. On the other hand, if you can become aware of your thoughts and feelings in the moment, you gain a powerful opportunity. You become the observer.

Step 2: Observe What's Going On—Inside and Out

AFTER BECOMING AWARE OF HOW YOU ARE FEELING, THINKING, OR acting, you can move to the next step of proactive change, which is to observe your thoughts and feelings. With awareness, you might say to yourself, "Oh, there are those feelings of frustration I get when I can't find a wheelchair. This is my opportunity to watch both the situation and my reaction to it."

If you catch yourself behaving impatiently, feeling frustrated, or experiencing some other emotion that you'd like to change, simply stop for a moment and observe what you're doing, saying, thinking or believing in that instant.

In the physical universe, the very act of observing something changes it. The science of quantum physics discovered that two researchers cannot view the same event and "see" the same thing. That which is being observed is altered by the consciousness of those who are observing it. The act of observing the mind begins to change the mind. This phenomenon offers a useful opportunity to create proactive change in your life and in healthcare.

Step 3: Make a Choice

AS YOU BECOME AWARE OF YOUR THOUGHTS AND BELIEFS THAT ARE triggering the behavior or experience you want to change—and can observe them—you reach a most powerful place: the place of choice. In this place you can choose to be frustrated or not. If you choose to be frustrated, great! Be really frustrated. Roll your eyes, stamp your foot and throw up your hands in exasperation. Whatever you do when you're really frustrated, do *more* of it. Really get worked up. You might be pleasantly surprised to discover what happens when you exaggerate the thing you're trying to change. Many times you'll begin to see your "frustrated routine" and that alone will take the edge off the experience. You might even laugh spontaneously as you see the humor in your "act."

You could also choose to be less frustrated (we'll talk about how to do that in a moment when we discuss the Mastery of Transformation). Either way, you win.

The simple process of becoming aware, observing your thoughts and beliefs (and your accompanying feelings) creates the option of choosing your actions. The more times you can *observe* the thoughts and emotions that normally cause your unwanted actions, and the more times you can *choose* your actions, the faster you will change.

Emotions—particularly those that are fear-based—are signals that call you to bring yourself into a state of heightened awareness. Whenever you become aware of a strong emotion, catch yourself in the moment, observe your feelings and behavior, and make a choice.

Whenever your mind runs on automatic pilot, there's no movement toward transforming your life. You—not your mind—must make the choices. Yet there are no right or wrong choices.

The important thing is to decide how you're going to be or what you're going to do. If you're angry, you can choose to identify with that emotion (*I'm* angry) or stop it. Always remember that choosing to change or choosing not to change is still a step in the right direction. At least you're making a conscious choice. As you will soon see, the choice itself is not as important as the process of making that choice.

The Mastery of Transformation

AFTER BECOMING AWARE OF YOUR THOUGHTS AND BELIEFS THAT ARE causing you to feel frustrated, the next step is to choose different thoughts and beliefs, as opposed to the fear-based ones that you want to change. Although greatly simplified here, this is the basis of the Mastery of Transformation.

When you become aware of frustrating or energy-draining thoughts, beliefs, and memories, you can choose new ones based in love rather than fear. Fear or love: there's always a choice.

Let's go back to our "no wheelchair" frustration and look at a new set of thoughts that might serve you better. You could choose to change your thoughts to something like the following:

No one is intentionally trying to make me angry by hiding wheelchairs. It's a systems problem. This may actually be a blessing. Maybe the delay in finding the wheelchair will prevent my patient or me from getting in an accident on the way home. Besides, this is a wonderful time to practice the Masteries of Awareness and Transformation. Actually, this whole experience is a gift. Thank you. Thank you. Thank you.

When you choose different, more loving thoughts, you're choosing to be less frustrated. As you choose thoughts that are based more in love, you will find yourself proactively changing, transforming yourself into a new, more authentic person. Still, it will take commitment and effort on your part. Status quo or a new you—it's your choice.

The Mastery of Intent

THE THIRD MASTERY IS THE MASTERY OF INTENT, WHICH IS REALLY THE mastery of energy. Quantum physics has shown that everything in the universe and on Earth is made up of energy. Objects we once thought were solid can be broken down into molecules, which are made up of atoms, which are made up of subatomic particles, which become nothing more than elements of energy. In other words, there are no solids; there is only energy in its many different forms.

When you master energy, you align yourself with the natural flow of the universe and the Higher Mind. When your mind is full of beliefs, thoughts and memories that come from love, your mind aligns with the creative power that makes the stars shine. Intent is true magic.

You can send intent—love—anywhere in the world at any time. You can send it through a thought or a prayer. You can send it through your eyes, your hands, a word, a touch. If you were to stop reading these words right now and send your intent to someone you didn't even know—maybe a person who is gravely ill in a hospital in another country—that person might very well heal more quickly. Prayer, meditation, caring, good thoughts and compassion have all been directly linked to accelerated healing. Meditation has been shown to change physical reality in reducing crime or casualties in war. It is the intent (energy) inherent in these activities that creates the healing or changes the physical reality.

Mastering the areas of Awareness, Transformation and Intent is not a destination; it is a never-ending life process. It must be practiced, reinforced and supported on a regular basis, optimally every day. In the next chapter, we will look at going beyond the Four Agreements with the introduction of "The New Agreements in Healthcare."

THE NEW AGREEMENTS
IN HEALTHCARE

When you are inspired by some great purpose, some extraordinary
project, all your thoughts break their bounds; your mind transcends
limitations, your consciousness expends in every direction, and you
find yourself in a new, great and wonderful world.

—Patanjali

IN LOOKING AT CHANGING THE WORKPLACE AND HEALTHCARE, IT SOON
became clear that the Four Agreements were, by themselves, not
enough to create and sustain change. I meditated for months asking
for guidance on what the missing pieces might be to create a comprehensive roadmap for both organizational and personal change.

Over the course of those months, I was given five additional
agreements that, when combined with the Four Agreements and
some other bodies of knowledge, provided the necessary ingredients
for sustainable change.

I wrote and published *The New Agreements in the Workplace: Releasing*
the Human Spirit in 2002, detailing those five new agreements. Some of

what you are about to read is included in *The New Agreements in the Workplace*. However just as every living being evolves, the New Agreements have also evolved. Much of that evolution resulted from practical application of the New Agreements in the real-world of healthcare.

The following are the New Agreements in Healthcare:

(1) Find Your Purpose

(2) Love, Grow and Serve Others

(3) Be a Systems Thinker

(4) Practice a Little Every Day

First New Agreement—Find Your Purpose

EACH OF US COMES INTO OUR LIFE EXPERIENCE FOR A PURPOSE—A LIFE purpose, a higher purpose. A part of each of us yearns to know and be aligned with our higher purpose. For many of us who have not yet discovered our purpose, life becomes a demonstration of what is most certainly *not* our life purpose. It is the feeling of being trapped in a life driven by obligation, habit and the expectations of others. It may well feel like a life that is long on stress and short on meaning.

Knowing and living one's life purpose creates meaning that transcends the humdrum of our normal wake-up, do-life, go-to-bed routine that constitutes the unexamined life. It appears that a deeper part of our humanity is awakening in many of us to ask, "What is my life purpose? What am I here to do?"

The answers to these profound questions are central to living a transformed life both at work and home—and to building great organizations. If you know your life purpose, universal creative energy conspires with you to bring your purpose to you. You become "attractive" to the circumstances in life that will allow you to live your life purpose.

An inner part of each of us knows our life purpose. I call this our Inner Wisdom. You might also call this all-knowing place inside each of us our Intuitive Knowing, Universal Knowing, Higher Self or Spirit. Many human beings go through life with an inner longing for meaning and purpose yet are too distracted by the outside rat race to explore the inner world where their life purpose awaits. We may be assured that there are no human beings on this planet whose life purpose is to get rich, get a better job or get their kids into Harvard. Nor is their life purpose to be poor, struggle to pay the rent or escape from a bad relationship. All of these things exist "out there" and are only an illusion of meaning and purpose, no matter how successful or unsuccessful we become.

A Spiritual Awakening to Life's True Purpose

I had the experience of living the American dream as the former owner of a successful business that brought a degree of wealth, prestige and security to me and my family. I had all the "stuff"—the big house, an expensive sports car, real estate, money in the bank and lots of friends who enjoyed the fact that I was probably overly generous and even foolish with my money. I had achieved everything I set out to do in the area of creating material wealth. Still, I felt empty and unfulfilled. I filled that emptiness with fast-living and alcohol. Then in 1980, I had a powerful spiritual awakening that changed everything.

To fully understand my spiritual awakening, it's important to know more about my life leading up to that point in time. I was born in 1945, a breech birth that nearly killed both my mother and me. Breech means butt first, which tends to give one a rather distorted first view of the world. I used this wrong way entrance into life as an excuse to justify my many mistakes.

At age two, asthma came wheezing into my bedroom late one night and became an unwanted guest for the next 14 years. Being small, scrawny and young for my grade, I was not highly regarded by my peers in those early years. I generally had the distinction of being picked last or not at all for team games which, given my skill level, was probably appropriate.

My dad was a tuna fisherman. Even though he didn't make much money and was gone a lot, I was proud of him. But it was my grandfather who became my guiding light. He didn't seem to see my many flaws that were so obvious to the rest of the world. I had the distinct feeling that he really liked spending time with me. Gramps always wanted me to spend weekends with him when I could. I couldn't wait for those special weekends.

Gramps was short, about five-feet-seven, even though he always claimed to be five-eight or five-nine. He was a wiry Scotsman and as strong as an ox. He feared no man. I heard stories about his prowess with a fist or an ax handle in the wild construction camps that he managed in his younger days. I heard the stories, but I never saw that side of my grandfather.

Sure, he was strong, yet what I most remember was that he encouraged me to do more than I thought I could do. He would say,

"You can do it, go ahead." He was gentle, too. He could tell when I needed an arm over my shoulder, a kind word, a hearty laugh.

We made a secret health breakfast that he called "musheshe" and "milkeke." Musheshe was a mixture of oats, eggs, and brewer's yeast cooked in a special pan that had seen better days. We ate it right out of the pan, much to my grandmother's chagrin. Milkeke was powdered whey, condensed milk and hot water. We never told anyone what the secret recipes were because it had taken Gramps so long to perfect them.

Gramp's dog, Jeep (a nondescript mutt, except for a face that always seemed to be smiling), was in charge of licking the pan, which she did very well. Gramps didn't believe in wasting anything and Jeep made sure the pan was spic-and-span. Then it was my job to wash up and put things in their proper place. Gramps always said, "A place for everything and everything in its place." That way we would have what we needed for tomorrow.

Gramps taught me to use his tools and took me to work with him. He could build or fix anything. Sadly, his mastery eluded me completely. Gramps didn't seem too concerned with my smashed-thumb, bent-nail, stripped-nut approach to building and fixing—as long as I made sure to clean up and put the tools where they belonged.

Becoming a "Little Man"

Gramps died when I was twelve. Although he didn't smoke or drink and was a health nut long before it became trendy, he died a terrible death, losing a protracted battle with cirrhosis of the liver. That tough old Scotsman went from a solid 165 pounds to a withered, yellow 100 pounds. We kids were not allowed to visit him in his last few weeks of life.

The day that Gramps died, I was sitting in his favorite chair. It was strange that I could smell him. I pounded the overstuffed, threadbare arm and watched as the dust danced in a silvery cloud among the sheer morning rays. I began to cry.

My grandmother walked stiffly into the room and barked, "You stop that crying. Your grandfather would never want to see you acting like that." I choked back the tears, wiped off my face, vowed not to cry again and went for a walk on the beach with Jeep.

Jeep looked for my grandfather every day. She would wait on the front porch by the flower pot, her usual lookout when my grandfather had to go somewhere without her, but Gramps never came home. Jeep would hear a sound and run to the door or into Gramp's room with determined hope. She always returned a little heavier than she left. I tried to cheer her up, play with her, take her on walks to the same places that we three amigos had always gone together, but it wasn't the same. Without Gramps, nothing would ever be the same.

She never stopped looking though Jeep must have known. She grew lethargic, suddenly old, and died a short time later. I really missed Jeep, too. But I didn't cry. I never cried much after Gramps died. Instead I started doing other things.

Shortly after my grandfather's death, I began to live life "on the edge." I started drinking alcohol at age 12, developing a "little man's complex," especially when I drank. I wanted to fight someone and sometimes it didn't matter if he was friend or foe. For awhile, it was humorous watching the "little man" looking more like a pinball than a partygoer. Then, I grew up and the fighting was no longer so comical. My friends stopped going to parties with me because I took the fun out of it for them. It seemed everywhere I went some sort of drama would break out.

Through college, marriage, family and starting my own business, I continued to live my life on the edge. I drank too much, drove too fast, played too hard, stayed out too late and punished myself in the name of living life to the fullest.

You Are Not Alone

One February morning in 1980, I found myself sitting alone on our family room couch, puzzling over the events of my life. That's when it happened.

Without warning, my grandfather appeared to me, standing across the room in his old maroon sweater with the holes in it. I could see through him, yet his image was as clear and as detailed as any living human being I have ever known.

I stopped breathing for a moment as a wave of fear surged through my body. Was I going insane? I burst into tears, unable to control the crying—crying that had been locked away in a twelve-year-old boy 22 years earlier. It didn't matter if I closed my eyes or buried my head in my hands, Gramps remained crystal clear.

After a few minutes, without a hint of judgment, he asked me a simple question. "David, what are you doing?"

I began to explain what it had been like when he died, how angry and hurt I had been. I told him how much I had loved him, missed him and how I wished I could have expressed my love to him when he was alive. I told him how Jeep had looked for him constantly, but then she died, too. Gramps slowly dissolved into the ethers. Shortly thereafter, I was able to compose myself somewhat.

Just when I thought this crazy episode was over, he appeared again. The tears cascaded again, this time in deep gratitude for all that he had done for me and how he had been there for me and, most especially, for revealing himself to me in my time of need. Gramps, the angel in the maroon sweater with the holes in it, smiled broadly and delivered the message that changed my life forever.

Wordlessly he said, "David, you are not alone," and then faded away, never to return.

In that instant, for possibly the first time in 22 years, I realized that I wasn't alone. I realized that I had never been alone. I realized that it was okay to cry—to feel and be fully human. I also realized that I was meant to teach. My life purpose was to be a teacher. Somehow I *knew* this simple truth.

In a period of ten minutes I went from being one kind of person to being someone very different. I gave up the fast-living that had become my life and began putting my now fraying marriage back together again. I vowed to be a better father.

Probably the most important thing that happened to me is that I found my life purpose. I became clear that I was here in this lifetime to wake up to my true nature and that I was to be a teacher or guide for others who also desired to discover and live their life purpose. Interestingly, I was to do this in the workplace, a place that was notoriously resistant to real change or outside-the-box thinking. Still it was my purpose, my dharma, my contribution to self and others in this lifetime.

It is the same for you and all human beings. We all have a life purpose. Once you know what your life purpose is, everything will change for you, too. Subtly you'll begin to see circumstances, events, people, meetings and material assistance begin to show up in your life to assist you in living your life purpose.

Will your life purpose come to you in a flash? Probably not. Even if you know your life purpose, there is still much work to do to make it a reality. You must build a bridge from today's reality to the new reality that is aligned with your life purpose.

Christine Builds a Bridge

The reality is that we have to pay the rent and our car payments or we will have some of life's learning experiences. To walk away from reality is irresponsible and almost always unnecessary. Instead, plan to build a bridge from your present reality to your new one, little by little. As Christine shares with us, "I chose to build my bridge plank by plank."

Two years ago, Christine was a successful manager with a high technology firm. She was good at her job, handsomely compensated and committed to the point of working whatever hours were necessary to "get the job done." Single and 36 years old, Christine lived alone, enjoying a healthy lifestyle along with a deep interest in spirituality and personal growth. She was open to, but felt it unlikely that she would meet a good man with similar values who was interested in a committed relationship. Although she kept busy, she was aware that something was missing from her life.

In a New Agreements visioning process, Christine saw herself

THE NEW AGREEMENTS IN HEALTHCARE

teaching the New Agreements principles in the workplace. This thought made her heart sing. She committed to work her way out of her job over a period of 18 months while learning as much as possible about New Agreements Healthcare. She would build a bridge from her current situation to her life purpose as a teacher in the workplace.

Christine made a choice to learn as much as possible and go deeply into this work. She became a Graduate Mentor for the New Agreements Teacher Training. She attended nearly every training and teleconference class and even accompanied me on a number of on-site consulting assignments, at her own expense. Linda and I worked one-on-one with Christine to help her balance the masculine and feminine aspects of her mind, which would allow her to pull a kindred-spirit man into her life. When things were difficult, we would laugh a lot together. Christine was committed to her vision. She was committed to her life. She was willing to practice every day and do the work that would make her vision real.

Today Christine is a New Agreements Consultant and a good one. She consults primarily in healthcare and models what she teaches. She is pulling her dream and life purpose to her. Along the way she met her "soul mate," a man who is a kindred spirit on his own spiritual path and is supportive of all that Christine is doing in her life. This is a prime example of what can happen when the power of commitment is combined with building a bridge to one's life purpose.

The power of intent and daily practice cannot be overstated in building this bridge. When we align with universal creative energy, life becomes easy and effortless. Christine stayed on purpose.

I think it's interesting to note that along the way to building this bridge, the ripple effect pulled a wonderful kindred spirit and companion into her life.

Second New Agreement—Love, Grow and Serve Others

THE WORKPLACE CAN BE THOUGHT OF AS A LIVING BEING IN THAT IT IS made up of people. Leaders, in particular, must integrate this universal principle into their leadership styles. As a leader, when you love your people, you'll love your work. When you grow your people by helping them increase their capabilities and expand their skill sets, you'll grow the business and enhance the performance of the organization. When you focus on loving and growing your people, they can focus on loving and serving your patients, your suppliers and each other. Lasting transformation in healthcare requires that caregivers care about *each other as fellow human beings.*

> *Of 139,380 former patients from 225 hospitals, the top two factors in determining Patient Satisfaction (PS) and patient's health outcomes were both directly related to Staff Interaction and PS directly correlated with Employee Satisfaction.*
>
> —Susan Frampton, Laura Gilpin and Patrick Charmel
> *Putting Patients First: Designing and Practicing Patient-Centered Care*

Of course, as you love, grow and serve others, you will love, grow and serve yourself in the process. There is a Sanskrit term called *Seva.* Seva means selfless service. It's said in some teachings that one can become a realized being through the sole practice of Seva.

This is a powerful agreement, especially for leaders and managers.

They will know that there is no greater gift they can give themselves than to contribute to others from a place of personal integrity and selfless service. As a leader in healthcare, at any level in the organization, if you can't care, you can't lead. This will be especially true in the changing environment that is coming to healthcare.

Imagine that in order to be an employee at your hospital, you were required to be a caring team player. Imagine that the leaders at all levels of your hospital practiced the art of selfless service to the caregivers they led and managed. An organization with this type of environment, energy and culture is literally vibrant. The amount of work, learning or healing (both physical and emotional) that can be accomplished in this working environment is mind-boggling.

Have you ever played on a team, participated in a charitable endeavor or taken part in a spiritual gathering that made you feel connected, joyous or even ecstatic? Maybe even people who were not part of the activities knew that there was something special about your group. In fact, I'll bet you remember that experience as one of the best of your life. Imagine work becoming this type of experience.

Achieving Critical Mass

An entire culture of a healthcare organization can be guaranteed to shift when a critical mass of executives and managers become champions of the transformation process. When the top five to ten percent of a hospital, including top management, *own* these new principles and are committed to the new vision, the entire culture will soon follow suit. It's no longer a matter of *if* the necessary changes can be achieved; it's a matter of *when*. As the thoughts, beliefs and actions of top and upper management shift, the culture of the organization literally begins to transform, despite resistance to change.

In real-world organizational change, we expect resistance to change. It's simply part of the process. Many times it's how we handle resistance that dramatically influences the speed of change.

Normally in the process of change, no good deed goes unpunished. By this I mean that the better the change process is working, the more resistance we can expect from those who are afraid of change. I call these caregivers who are afraid of change the *Nay-Sayers*. It's not unusual to see Nay-Sayers exhibit various levels of resistance (from passive to passive-aggressive to even overt refusal to go along with the changes leadership wants to make). Leaders must avoid putting too much attention on the Nay-Sayers.

It is a universal principle that whatever we put our attention and energy on *grows*. If you put your attention on something, it will begin to create or recreate beliefs in your mind that support that which you are putting your attention on. With time, our attention controls our belief. The more energy leadership expends placating Nay-Sayers, the slower the change process will go.

This is not to say that resisters should be jettisoned outright. Every caregiver should be given an opportunity to participate in the change process, to learn and to grow. However, when it is clear that Nay-Sayers are not going to be members of the team and positive influences to others in the change process, they must be assisted out of the organization.

It is actually good leadership and a compassionate action to move a caregiver from an organization where he is unhappy. Unhappy people drag everyone down. Many times when negative people leave the organization, it's a matter of addition by subtraction.

Third New Agreement—Be a Systems Thinker

BEFORE WE CAN TALK ABOUT THE TRANSFORMATION OF HEALTHCARE AS we know it, we must explore the incredible world of systems, systems theory and systems thinking. Before completing this discussion, we will take something that might be seen as complex and make it elegantly simple. Let's start by looking at the big universal picture through the lens of physics and quantum physics.

The observable universe is one very large system. Within this system are large subsystems that might be described as clusters of galaxies, massive clouds of gas and other extremely large features. Within these features are more massive subsystems, such as galaxies like our Milky Way, which lead to individual star systems such as our solar system, which have subsystems we might call planets, including the home of all humanity that we call Earth.

Earth, of course, is made up of many smaller subsystems, which contain ecosystems in the form of natural and manmade systems that we might define as the workplace or a business. Healthcare, including the delivery of healthcare, is a function of systems and subsystems, all the way from government-mandated Medicare to how we register a patient at Gila Regional Medical Center. It's important to realize this because the physical universe is made up entirely of systems (and subsystems) and everything (and I do mean *everything!*) is connected. Nothing happens in any part of physical reality that does not have some effect on the rest of the systems.

A clear understanding of the critical role that systems play (in the healthcare experience that we, as caregivers, create for both our patients and ourselves) is a necessary component of any change effort. Why? Because systems dictate the vast majority of the results we experience. It is a well-documented fact that more than 90 percent of the results we produce in the workplace are a function of the systems in which people work, *not* the efforts of the people. This tells us that if we wish to produce better patient care at lower cost, we must address upgrading the current systems that produce the results we want to improve.

Sadly, most leaders who are responsible for improving healthcare organizations are not aware of the powerful role that systems play in providing healthcare services—both the good and the not-so-good. Instead, leaders might look at cutting costs by mandating reduction of full-time employees (FTEs), cutting benefits or services, or hollowing out the organization in some other way.

These leaders, for the most part are not doing things this way because they are bad or unintelligent people. Most are certainly highly intelligent, good people who are doing the things they have learned to do which may have worked at some level in the past. However, there's a much more effective, elegant approach to transforming healthcare that reduces costs while improving patient and caregiver satisfaction. Think systems. Make the systems visible. Improve the systems. Be a systems-based leader/manager.

What Is a System?

This question is asked of me more often than any other when I present New Agreements Healthcare. Systems are also called processes. Systems are how we do things or how things get done.

For instance, at Gila Regional we found that often nurses could not find a wheelchair to transport a patient. In addition, it was not unusual that even when a wheelchair was located, it might be missing critical pieces, like footrests. Although it was informal, a system was in place at Gila Regional that virtually guaranteed that this situation would continue to be a problem. Because the problem was not seen as a function of an informal system that wasn't working well (but rather as a "people" problem), there was little that could be done to resolve the situation. Worst of all, people pointed fingers at each other, sniped behind other's backs or became outright angry at not having what they needed to take good care of their patients. Sound familiar?

Until we begin to think in terms of systems being at the heart of everything that is happening in any organization, we naturally tend to think that people are causing the problems and frustrations. In most cases this is simply not true. Yes, people at Gila were hiding wheelchairs so they would have one if they needed it. However, the problem is not the people who are trying to work around a less-than-robust system; the problem is with the system.

Once we examined the wheelchair issue in a systems-based way, it quickly became apparent that some wheelchairs should be retired, some refurbished, some new ones purchased and some special poles installed so that they would remain in their proper area and not be stolen when wheeled to the parking lot. The proper actions were taken and the problem was solved. More important-ly, improving this system opened up lines of communication between nursing, maintenance, purchasing and volunteers that had previously been tenuous at best around the wheelchair issue.

For those of you who want to explore a system a little closer to home, I recommend looking at how you brush your teeth. Although you probably don't think a great deal about how you brush your teeth, you have created a system for doing so. It's an informal system, but a system nonetheless. Because you brush your teeth automatically every day, the system you have created is invis-ible to you.

For those of us who aren't systems thinkers, the vast majority of systems that circumscribe our lives, both at work and at home, are invisible. We just don't see them. To make the system you use for brushing your teeth visible, I suggest brushing with your other hand. Really. Try it tomorrow morning and notice all the actions you've been doing automatically with your normal brushing hand.

KISS

You may have heard of the KISS concept that stands for "Keep It Simple, Stupid." I think KISS might have been created for systems work and really stands for "Keep It Systems Simple."

Having studied a number of the foremost systems experts in the field, I found that they are brilliant engineers, scientists, statisticians and mathematicians. Yet when we teach even the most basic con-cepts to people who are new to systems-improvement work, it is not unusual for them to feel intimidated, fearing that they might not be able to understand or use these generally accepted principles and systems-improvement tools.

With a little inspiration from Spirit, we have been able to simplify systems improvement work to the point where any caregiver can be successful and make patient care better. Most importantly, it makes our work in healthcare more satisfying and meaningful. Even for people for whom English is a second language, these New Agreements principles, tools, and techniques are easy to learn and apply. This benefit will become increasingly relevant as the nursing shortage grows and, to fill the gap, more caregivers are attracted from countries outside the US.

The following three simple New Agreements Systems Principles are what you need to know to become a systems whiz.

90/10 – 90 percent of the results being created in the workplace are a function of the systems in which people work, *NOT* the efforts of the people. To improve results, we must optimize the systems in which we and our people work.

80/20 – 80 percent of the results are created by 20 percent of the variables. Focus your efforts on improving the critical 20 percent to make the most difference. If you would like to test this 80/20 theory at home, look in your closet and you'll see that 80 percent of the time you wear 20 percent of the clothes in your closet. Or make a list of all the restaurants at which you dine. You will find that about 80 percent of the time you eat at 20 percent of the restaurants on your list.

Since there is never enough time to fix everything (nor should we attempt to do so), we must focus on the critical 20 percent of the issues that will give us 80 percent of the improvements we seek. This gives the highest return on our efforts and investments.

50/50 – The two critical factors to improving any organization are (1) transforming systems, and (2) transforming (loving and growing) people. Both are equally important and create an integrated whole. For change to be sustainable, *BOTH* must happen together. If you work only on improving systems, the people will often sabotage your systems-improvement efforts. If you work only on growing people or creating teamwork, people may feel better about themselves, but the results will remain essentially the same. Soon, even good feelings will be undone by poor or status quo systems.

That's it—90/10, 80/20, and 50/50. These three simple principles are everything you'll need to know to create a foundation for your systems work. Next we'll look at the simple tools that anyone can use to make systems visible, identify the critical 20 percent of the variables and optimize the systems to create better results. In addition, we'll compare New Agreements Systems Tools and Techniques with the more traditional problem-solving modalities in healthcare.

Oh No! Not More-Better-Different

Knowing that we have problems is one thing. Knowing how to solve those problems is quite another. A nearly universal approach to problem solving in healthcare is *more-better-different*. The more-better-different model includes doing *more* of what's not working, doing what's not working *better* and doing what's not working *differently*.

The best we can hope for with this rarely questioned approach is marginal improvement. Many times this approach creates unintended consequences, making things worse rather than better. For many leaders and managers, this approach appears to be the only alternative. It's all they know. But, are we beating a dead horse? Let's have a little fun while we attempt to answer that question.

Commonsense advice from knowledgeable horse trainers includes the following two highly recommended adages:

(1) It's best to ride the horse in the direction it's going, and

(2) If the horse you are riding dies, get off.

Seems reasonable enough. Yet, it appears that horse sense may be lacking in many of our dead-end, more-better-different approaches to dealing with dead horses. Old more-better-different solutions may include the following:

(1) Buy a stronger whip

(2) Try a new bit or bridle

(3) Switch riders

(4) Move the horse to a new location

(5) Ride the horse for longer periods of time

(6) Say things like, "This is the way we have always ridden this horse."

(7) Appoint a committee to study the horse

(8) Arrange to visit other sites where they ride dead horses more efficiently

(9) Increase the standards for riding dead horses

(10) Create a test for measuring our riding ability

(11) Compare how we are riding now with how we did it ten or twenty years ago

(12) Complain about the state of horses these days

(13) Come up with a new style of riding

(14) Blame the horse's parents. The problem is often in the breeding

(15) Tighten the cinch

Thanks to Sue Albert, we have this humorous description of educators' problem-solving approaches to fixing education, which can also be applied to the "dead horse" that healthcare has become.

Making Invisible Systems Visible

I believe that one major reason we have been so resistant to new ways of problem solving is that the tools and techniques appear daunting to many. This is especially true for traditional systems-improvement tools.

The most basic, traditional systems improvement tools (such as flow charts, run charts, control charts, fishbone diagrams, scatter diagrams, affinity diagrams, Pareto analysis and others), are intimidating to many newcomers to the world of systems improvement. When people are afraid, it is much more difficult for them to learn and apply new concepts and tools. While thinking through ways to make systems improvement tools simple, easy to use, and even fun, a whole new way to address systems improvement emerged. These are New Agreements Systems-Improvement Tools and Techniques. Here's how they work:

Form a team that includes the "right" people (should be voluntary, if possible). Virtually any system can be improved and kept sustainable using the following "low tech" tools and techniques. You will need the following items:

Flip chart
Colored markers (nontoxic)
Three colors of Post-It™ brand notes
Red dots (stick-on type)
Masking tape (one-inch minimum)
A trained New Agreements facilitator (internal, if possible)

When working on a new project, the facilitator will usually start with a facilitated *emotional content* brainstorm. People most often join a systems-improvement team because they are frustrated with something that's going on in the hospital and they want to do something about it. Before we can work systems issues, we must get the emotional energy out of the people and "on the wall."

For example, when we started looking at fixing the registration system at Gila Regional, we first had to deal with the strong emotions and frustrations of the people on the team. Different departments were pointing fingers at each other and, in some cases, refusing to talk with each other. Contrary to traditional wisdom, this type of emotion is very positive. It shows that people care. Many times the people who are most frustrated become the biggest champions for implementing these change processes.

An emotional content brainstorm gets the emotional energy out of people and on the wall (flip chart). It's amazing how these types of brainstorms start with people jumping up and down, expressing strong emotions and being quite animated. As people see their concerns going up on the flip chart, the energy begins to settle down. Finally, when people cannot think of anything we've missed, the room becomes quiet and we're ready to go to the next steps.

Once we've handled the emotional energy, we can begin putting the systems in question on the wall (making it visible) using Post-It™ notes.

Each of the three colors of notes represents issues that fall into one of three categories. One color is the functions involved in a particular system. Another color represents the problems within a particular function within the system (more detailed). The third color represents broad problems that cut across the entire system, such as lack of training, lack of resources or a lack of information technology infrastructure.

As we ask the team about the problems they see in the existing system, it is not unusual for the group to become quite excited and vocal when relating certain issues. If there is enough emotional energy coming from the group, we will put a red dot on the offending sticky. High emotional content is a strong indication of systems problems. Also, strong emotional energy is an accurate indicator of an issue that falls into the critical 20 percent of the system that is producing 80 percent of the problems.

For instance, if 100 Post-It™ notes land on the flip chart, we expect that 20 will have red dots (the 80/20 rule). Once we have the whole system on the wall, it is usually quite apparent to the group where the problems lie and where to begin the work of upgrading the system. I might add that it is most of the time shocking and somewhat humorous for people to see "how we have been doing things." It is important that we not judge anything that's been done in the past, but rather focus on the future. It is also imperative that we have a little fun along the way. We do our best work when we have fun, laugh often, and enjoy each other's company.

Put It on the Wall

I cannot stress enough that the *only* way you will be able to make a system visible is to PUT IT ON THE WALL. Putting a system on the wall means using brainstorming, Post-It™ notes and red-dots-on-the-flip-chart techniques as described above. You cannot see a system using more traditional approaches.

You can't take copious notes, watch slide presentations, listen to the boss (or any other expert), put information on a white board or an illustrator, or pass out detailed reports. Unless the building is burning down, you must PUT IT ON THE WALL. This goes not only for process improvement meetings, but executive and management meetings, too. If you are weary of committee-like meetings that are unproductive, begin conducting meetings using these tools and techniques and watch what happens. Your ability to have effective meetings in a fraction of the time will emerge. And the driver of every meeting should be *action*.

Action Items

Every systems-improvement meeting must create Action Items. Action Items are little actions that the team determines must be taken to move the improvement process forward. An Action Item requires three elements. They are (1) the action to be taken, (2) the person or persons who will be accountable for completing the action, and (3) the date by which the action will be completed. It's most important that the Action Items become the agenda for the following meeting. In general, try never to leave a meeting without documenting action items.

Healing Relationships

Although we do not normally think about systems-improvement work as being a healing environment for relationships among the people doing the work, when facilitated properly, it is an unusually powerful healing environment. Relationships, sometimes the most disagreeable ones, are transformed from fear, anger and frustration to love, support and respect. People on these teams see that the issues, problems and miscommunications they have been experiencing with each other and other departments are a result of poor systems—not their coworkers deliberately making life difficult.

When team members see that poor systems make it virtually impossible for fellow caregivers to do better, real compassion and understanding emerges. The finger-pointing, gossip and back-stabbing simply go away. We watch combatants from different departments come together with deeper levels of trust, compassion, understanding and camaraderie over and over again.

In addition, there is something special about being on a team that is doing something meaningful. New Agreements Healthcare also encourages us to grow as human beings. The opportunity to heal ourselves as individuals and expand our consciousness makes its presence known to us in the process. I believe that all organizations would benefit if they aspired to create this energetic dynamic within their teams and work groups. At Gila Regional, people looked forward to attending systems-improvement meetings as a way to reconnect, receive support and encouragement, and expand the human experience in the workplace.

Fourth New Agreement—Practice a Little Every Day

REALIZING LIFE PURPOSE AND ATTAINING CERTAIN LEVELS OF LIFE MASTERY requires practice. It's the same for organizations. If we desire to learn something new and make this new skill set a part of how we operate in the world, the organization must create and maintain a practice. The most effective practice is done every day. For example, if you want to make the New Agreements real in your organization, you will need to practice using the tools that make these powerful Agreements real. Practice doesn't have to be arduous. Actually, we do our best practice when we are inspired or having fun.

Practices to consider when implementing New Agreements Healthcare might include the following:

The Masteries: As a foundation for individual caregivers, we highly recommend practicing the Masteries described earlier in this book. The Masteries are designed to allow human beings to be proactive in creating the life experience to which they aspire.

Meditate: We strongly recommend meditating twice a day, *every* day for 30 minutes. If you're new to meditation, start with five minutes once a day *every* day and work your way into it. Soon your daily meditations will become like brushing your teeth. You won't feel complete leaving the house or going to bed without the stress relief and calm of your daily meditation.

Use Systems Tools: Use them every day. Don't have a meeting without a flip chart, Post-It™ notes and red dots at the ready.

Be Data-Driven: Whenever anyone comes to you with a problem or suggestion, ask for the data that supports their point of view. You'll find that most problems and opinions not supported by good data are inaccurate or simply wrong. As systems guru W. Edwards Deming so eloquently admonishes, "In God we trust. Everyone else must use data."

In healthcare today, there's a big push to become "evidence-based." Being evidence-based is the same as being data-driven. In response to reported problems, the first question out of the mouth of a good leader or manager should be, "Where is the data to support your opinion or conclusion?" It is amazing how often the nature of a perceived problem changes when data is collected to define the problem. Many times the problem simply goes away. It never existed except in the mind of the perceiver.

Be Kind: What we put out comes back. If we are kind and compassionate, we will tend to draw kindness and compassion to ourselves. Conversely, if we are unkind, mean-spirited or angry, we will tend to pull those types of negative people and circumstances to ourselves. The Dalai Lama says that his religion is kindness. Most certainly the essence of the teachings of Jesus revolved around the embodiment of kindness, compassion and unconditional love.

Do the Right Thing: You will have many opportunities to choose between doing the easy thing and the right thing. The easy road becomes the hard road. The fast road becomes the slow road. Look in your heart and then do the right thing. This practice is so important for leaders at all levels of the organization. If there is a battle between your head and your heart in identifying the right thing, trust your heart.

Remove the Dead Moose: Most organizations have a laundry list of long-term problems that have existed in the organization *forever,* but which no one has the courage to address. I call these types of problems "Dead Moose in the middle of the room." Big, stinky, Dead Moose problems that people have been dancing around forever. Usually these are people issues. I know you know what I'm talking about. With the Dead Moose (as with all fear-based situations), the truth only hurts once. The lies go on and on.

Stand for Something Meaningful: It may take a while to find your life purpose, but once you do, stand in your truth.

Build Your Bridge Every Day: Take a little step toward your life purpose every day. Great journeys are made by putting one foot in front of the other in each moment. Great life achievements are created by taking little actions every day.

Do a Little Every Day: Practice your new skills and use your new tools in a sensible manner. Don't try to do too much. Strive for consistency. Incorporate these practices into your life in a way that gives you the best chance to stay on course every day. For example, if you're going to start meditating, start out slowly. Then gradually increase your time as you get better at the practice.

Be Brave: You will have detractors and challenges. The better your work, the more detractors and challenges will come your way. It is this way with all true leaders. Expect it. Transcend everything with courage, honor, humanity, humility and grace. A hearty laugh is good for the soul, too.

Have Gratitude: Life, even when it's challenging, is a gift. In meditation I was shown a simple mantra that has proved to be a wonderful practice for remembering to stay in gratitude. The mantra is "Thank you, Thank you, Thank you." I introduced this mantra as a practice for students in the Teacher Training and this simple practice is changing lives.

When you would normally say thanks, try saying, "Thank you, Thank you, Thank you." Watch what happens both in you and in the person you thank. When a person cuts you off on the road, say or think, "Thank you, Thank you, Thank you." This simple practice will change your life and enhance the lives of the people you touch.

Love Comprehensively: Remember that you can't love others more than you love yourself. You must take care of yourself first (not in an egocentric way). In the world of healthcare and the workplace, it is an act of self-love to not allow others to take advantage of you. Remove yourself from unsolvable situations that demean you. When in doubt, look for kindness, compassion and respect as your guiding principles.

Daily practice of these guiding principles will keep you on track with New Agreements Healthcare.

In our quest to blend the best body-mind-spirit approaches to modern healthcare delivery, we found a model already exists and appears to deliver the goods. In Chapter 5 we "bring in the clowns" and so much more with the heroes and champions of Planetree.

PLANETREE:
A COMPASSIONATE, WORKABLE
COMPLEMENT FOR A NEW AMERICAN
HEALTHCARE SYSTEM

Surgeons must be very careful
When they take the knife!
Underneath their fine incisions
Stirs the Culprit— Life!

—Emily Dickinson

TOM PETERS, ONE OF AMERICA'S FOREMOST MANAGEMENT GURUS and a strong advocate for healthcare reform, calls Planetree, "a radical model for new healthcare/healing/health/wellness excellence." I agree with his statement, except for the word *radical*.

I don't believe Planetree is radical except when compared to the current mindset that dominates healthcare today. Planetree is much more commonsense than it is radical if you refer to the reliable data that's widely available on the power of healing environments. For a model that healthcare in America can aspire to, you need look no further than Planetree.

When I first began working with Gila Regional, I was unaware of the powerful practice and philosophy for healthcare organizations called Planetree. That soon changed. As a Planetree hospital affiliate, Gila Regional worked diligently to implement Planetree practices and principles. The more I learned about Planetree, the more I gravitated toward it. Most, if not all, of the foundational practices and principles of Planetree resonated with the universal principles that comprise New Agreements Healthcare.

The attitude that drives the Planetree philosophy is best articulated by Planetree President, Susan Frampton and her co-authors Laura Gilpin and Patrick Charmel in their book, *Putting Patients First: Designing and Practicing Patient-Centered Care.*

> "There is a misconception that supportive interactions require more staff or more time and are therefore more costly. Although labor costs are a substantial part of any hospital budget, the interactions themselves add nothing to the budget. Kindness is free. Listening to patients or answering their questions costs nothing. It can be argued that negative interactions—alienating patients, being non-responsive to their needs or limiting their sense of control—can be very costly. . . . Angry, frustrated or frightened patients may be combative, withdrawn and less cooperative—requiring far more time than it would have taken to interact with them initially in a positive way."

Planetree is about human beings caring for and serving other human beings. This involves providing nurturing, compassionate, personalized care to patients and families. Just as important is how the staff cares for themselves and each other and how organizations create cultures that support and nurture their staffs. Experiential staff retreats that sensitize staff to hospital experiences from the patient's perspective better enable them to holistically serve patients. The Planetree care model encourages healing partnerships between patients, family members and caregivers, enabling patients to be active participants in their healthcare. The following nine Planetree practices anchor its philosophy.

(1) The Importance of Human Interaction

(2) Informing and Empowering Diverse Populations: Consumer Health Libraries and Patient Information

(3) Healing Partnerships: The Importance of Including Friends and Family

(4) Nutrition: The Nurturing Aspect of Food

(5) Spirituality: Inner Resources for Healing

(6) Human Touch: The Essentials of Communicating—Caring through Massage

(7) Healing Arts: Nutrition for the Soul

(8) Integrating Complementary and Alternative Practices into Conventional Care

(9) Healing Environments: Architecture and Design Conducive to Health

Architectural Design Conducive to Health and Healing

PLANETREE BELIEVES THAT THE PHYSICAL ENVIRONMENT IS VITAL TO THE healing process of the patient. Facility design includes efficient layouts that support patient dignity and personhood, featuring domestic aesthetics, art and warm home-like atmospheres. Noninstitutional designs that value humans, not just technology, are emphasized while architectural barriers that inhibit patient control and privacy (or interfere with family participation) are removed. A heightened awareness of the symbolic messages communicated by design is essential.

Healing environments are just as essential for the staff as it is for patients. Physicians, nurses and ancillary staff are equally affected by the environment, so lounges and sacred space for staff are an important component in creating Planetree healing environments.

Importance of the Nutritional and Nurturing Aspects of Food

NUTRITION IS AN INTEGRAL PART OF HEALTH AND HEALING, ESSENTIAL NOT only for good health, but also as a source of pleasure, comfort and familiarity. Scientific data demonstrates the role of nutrition in health and disease, so Planetree healthcare facilities are responsible role models for delicious, healthy eating.

Patient and Family Education

THE PLANETREE MODEL EMPHASIZES PATIENT AND FAMILY EDUCATION through customized information packets, collaborative care conferences and patient pathways. An open chart policy enables patients to read and write in their medical records. A self-medication program allows patients to keep their medications at the bedside and assume responsibility for their administration.

Social Support Vital to Good Health

MORE MEDICAL AND SOCIAL RESEARCHERS FIND THAT ANYTHING THAT promotes a sense of love and intimacy, connection and community is healing. Planetree supports and encourages involvement of family and significant others whenever possible. The Care Partner Program provides education and training to assist family participation in caring for patients while hospitalized and at home after discharge. Significant others make valuable contributions to the quality of a patient's hospital experience and volunteer care partners are available for patients who are alone.

One such program (the volunteer hand-holding program) trains volunteers to provide emotional support by accompanying patients having minor surgery into the operating room. Another element of the Planetree Model is unrestricted visiting hours, even in the ICU.

Planetree recognizes how vital spirituality is in healing the whole person. Supporting patients, families and staff in connecting with their own inner resources creates a more healing environment. Chapels, gardens and meditation rooms provide spaces for reflection and prayer, and chaplains are vital members of the healthcare team.

The Healing Power of Touch

TOUCH IS ESSENTIAL FOR COMMUNICATING CARING AND IT'S OFTEN missing from clinical settings. Planetree makes therapeutic full-body or chair massage available for patients, families and staff. Internship programs for massage therapists and training for volunteers to give hand and foot rubs are available and help keep costs minimal. As part of the Care Partner Program, families can be taught to give massages to loved ones while in the hospital and at home. Nurses, doctors and staff use chair massage focusing on the neck, shoulders and back to relieve stress or re-energize.

Involving the Creative Power of Soul

PLANETREE CREATES AN ATMOSPHERE OF SERENITY AND PLAYFULNESS using music, storytellers, clowns and funny movies. Artwork in patient rooms, treatment areas and on art carts enhance the ambiance. Volunteers work with patients to create art while involvement from artists, musicians, poets and story tellers from the community help expand the boundaries of healthcare facilities.

A Role for Complementary/Alternative Medicine

COMPLEMENTARY AND ALTERNATIVE MEDICAL (CAM) THERAPY USE HAS increased in the last decade. This trend will continue to grow in the coming years. Some individuals choose these therapies because these healthcare alternatives are more congruent with their beliefs, values and philosophical orientations toward health and life. It is important to realize a growing number of people desire treatment options that complement more conventional medical approaches.

The calming effect of aromatherapy is now being used on agitated patients during MRIs and with geropsychiatric patients. Pet therapy has been successfully implemented in Planetree hospitals to provide beneficial effects to patients, including mood elevation, enhanced social interaction and lowered blood pressure.

Planetree affiliates instituted heart disease reversal programs and mind/body medicine interventions (such as meditation and healing guided imagery, therapeutic massage, therapeutic touch, Reiki, acupuncture, Tai Chi and yoga) to meet growing patient demand for CAM therapies.

While Planetree affiliation is not necessary to create a powerful transformation with New Agreements Healthcre, I highly recommended that it be considered. Being a Planetree affiliate tells a lot about the mindset of leadership in a healthcare organization. If leadership is more about numbers than about the people (patients and caregivers), then neither Planetree nor New Agreeents Healthcare will be effective. Frankly, if leadership doesn't care about people, organizational transformation in healthcare is probably impossible.

I personally cannot emphasis enough the importance of leaders in healthcare being driven by the awareness that *patient satisfaction* is a function of *caregiver satisfaction*. If you want to take better care of your patients, take better care of your caregivers *first*.

The Planetree philosophy aligns with New Agreements Healthcare philosophy in that we believe that the best way to become patient-centered is to focus on loving, growing and serving caregivers who will, in turn, love and care for their patients.

The two most important factors in loving, growing and serving the caregivers are (1) improve the systems in which caregivers work so they can be successful in delivering quality care to their patients, and (2) provide them with skilled, caring, systems-based leadership, management and supervision. If we, as healthcare leaders, commit to these two basic principles of more enlightened leadership, we position all concerned—ourselves, our patients and our caregivers—to feel well cared for. Put into the simplest terms, I believe the charter of every leader in healthcare is to *fix the systems* and *love, grow and serve the caregivers.* Of course, this includes creating healing environments for both patients and caregivers.

Yet we live in an environment that requires financial performance from healthcare. It is important that improvements to healthcare organizations be real, measurable *and* positively influence the bottom line.

Results and performance are keys to the survival of American healthcare organizations during the transition from *what we have been* to *what we must become.* As it turns out, caring about people and improving the bottom line are actually joined at the hip. Chapter 6 presents "New Agreements Healthcare in Action" and how to significantly improve the healthcare bottom line in these perilous economic times.

NEW AGREEMENTS HEALTHCARE IN ACTION

Why not learn by getting down to actual practice?
—Mohandas K. Gandhi

WITH THE SIGNIFICANT INVESTMENT THAT GILA REGIONAL HAD MADE to Planetree both structurally and emotionally, CEO John Rossfeld, didn't want to start over with a new program. Instead, he required that New Agreements Healthcare work synergistically with Planetree and accelerate the process of implementing their principles and practices. The New Agreements Healthcare program in conjunction with Planetree would be called, "Planetree—The Next Steps."

To kick off the program, we believed that the one area where we could bring the most value to the hospital was in the area of recreating and optimizing systems within the hospital, physicians' offices and, in some cases, the community. We would start work in the hospital patient-registration system, which had much to be desired.

In fact, Gila Regional had been working for almost three years, attempting to fix the problems in Registration with little or no success. Most thought that Registration at Gila Regional was getting worse instead of better.

John Rossfeld actually chuckled as he spoke the words, "If you can fix Registration, we'll know this New Agreements stuff works." As it turned out, "New Agreements stuff" *did* work.

The nine-month progress report that follows gives details about how New Agreements Healthcare was implemented and the results presented to the leadership of Gila Regional.

New Agreements Healthcare Hospital Improvement Report for the Nine Months Ending March 31, 2006

Introduction: Beginning June 1, 2005, GRMC contracted with New Agreements, Inc. to guide implementation of a comprehensive hospital improvement plan based upon New Agreements Healthcare and Planetree Patient–Centered Care principles.

Prior to the June 1 start date of the one-year contract between GRMC and New Agreements, Inc., some work was initiated to improve the Patient Registration Process at GRMC. The team that was first created to address problems in the Registration Process at GRMC was called the Patient Access Management Team or PAM for short. A New Agreements systems-based approach was employed by the PAM team, which was guided and facilitated by David Dibble and New Agreements, Inc. staff.

Systems-Based Implementation

At GRMC, as in all organizations, everything (one system) is connected to everything else (other systems), forming an interconnected network of systems. Nothing happens in isolation. As expected, PAM soon found itself involved not only with Registration, but other functions as well. As a result, other teams were formed to address problems that were in some way connected to Registration. As time went on, other important improvement opportunities presented themselves and action was taken to seize those opportunities, too. This document is a report of the progress made to date and the status of ongoing improvement efforts at GRMC within the general context of New Agreements Healthcare and Planetree.

It should be made clear that virtually all of the improvements experienced to date and those GRMC will experience in the future are or will be a result of the hard work of a growing group of dedicated caregivers who want to learn and grow and be active contributors to building a better GRMC. It is suggested that if readers of this report have questions concerning the results noted in this document, they go to the source of these improvements, the magnificent caregivers of GRMC who have done this remarkable work.

This report begins with descriptions of the history and methods used by specific New Agreements Process Improvement Teams. In some cases, because of the relatively small sample sizes in some of the data collected, one each of the highest and lowest scores were eliminated from the data to avoid skewing the results.

New Agreements Process Improvement Team History and Methodology

Context for Creating a New Agreements Systems-Improvement Team: All teams are comprised of volunteers who are trained in the use of New Agreements Systems-Improvement Tools and Techniques, which include facilitation, meeting rules, brainstorming, Post-It™ notes, red dots, systems-improvement principles (90/10, 80/20 and 50/50), action items, documentation, and personal/team accountability. Please note that it is not unusual for some team members to leave the teams for various reasons during the life of a team or for new members to join a team after the start date. When important information resides outside the teams, non-permanent "guests" are invited to attend meetings to share valuable data and create buy-in for actions that will affect various caregivers or departments.

PAM/Registration Team

The Previous Condition: Registration was a department in turmoil. Morale was very low and there was an adversarial relationship and little communication between Registration and the Business Office. Performance of the department was poor and frustration was evident in the department and with people who had to deal with Registration. Mistakes made in Registration leveraged into other areas of the hospital, frustrating caregivers in the hospital and in physician's offices. Constant firefights drove up costs and adversely affected both patient and caregiver satisfaction. Turnover in the department was excessive.

The Registration system was put "on the wall" where, for the first time, it was made visible for all to see. Once visible, the system was broken down so that, for the first time, it could be understood. Once understood, the critical 20 percent of the variables that were driving 80 percent of the problems were identified and action was taken to resolve the issues.

Actions Taken by PAM and Spin-Off Teams

- It was determined that there were 46 categories of mistakes being made creating approximately 500 registration mistakes over the period examined. The PAM team identified the "Big Nine" categories of errors that were accounting for approximately 400 of the 500 registration errors (80/20 systems principle). The team began work to eliminate the Big Nine.

- Created a formal, best-practices training program and manual for all Registration personnel

- Replaced the embosser system with a new "label/wristband" system of patient identification

- Created a new standardized Registration Form that could be used by both GRMC and in Physician's Offices

- Recovered charges being denied because of missing, inaccurate or wrong data

- Established open communication between Registration and the Business Office caregivers

Results Indicated by the Actions of PAM and Spin-Off Teams

(**Note:** Press-Ganey patient satisfaction scores are a lagging indicator of caregiver satisfaction. Press-Ganey and most other scores lag real-time improvement and it is expected that the 2006 figures listed herein will act as new baseline metrics going forward. It is expected that as caregiver satisfaction rises, patient satisfaction will begin to rise in the first quarter of 2007 along with a reduction in historic turnover rates.)

The two controllable factors that most influence caregiver satisfaction are (1) the opportunity to be successful in the job by working in good systems, and (2) skilled caring and systems literate leadership/ management/ supervision. These two controllable factors are a focus of the New Agreements work being done at Gila Regional.

The Teams

Frontline Shooters Team—Interviewed all of the registration caregivers to get their inputs on the current condition of the department. In addition, the team created online Medical Terminology and Dictionaries as tools and support for Registration caregivers.

No Train-No Gain Team—A ten-part comprehensive training manual was created for training and testing competency of people who must register patients at GMRC (see Registration Training Manual). This training manual design is a model for training manuals for other GRMC departments.

Modern Millie's Team—Replaced dumb terminals in Registration with needed PCs and identified other technology upgrades and tools to support the registration processes. Result: All Registration personnel have the tools they need to do the job efficiently and correctly. Printers are still a problem, but the team is working to resolve operational issues. When operational issues are resolved, each caregiver registering patients will have his/her own dedicated printer, a significant savings that will reduce time and mistakes in the printing cycle.

COMM Team—Looked at the critical data that is needed to register patients both at GRMC and from Physician's Offices. Created a new Registration Form in partnership with physician offices. The new form included training and FAQ documents. When physician offices used the new form correctly, error rates dropped from 80 percent to 5 percent. The form continues to evolve with the mandatory inclusion of ABNs and Lab information and with online registration scheduled to go live with the new standardized form. This will significantly improve the registration process for both Physician's Offices and GRMC and reduce or eliminate denials due to no prior authorizations or missing/wrong CPT codes.

Blue Card Team—Of all the legacy systems that caused high levels of frustration for both people in Registration and others who had to use it, the embosser system was the biggest offender. The Blue Card Team created a new system that utilized printed labels and wristbands to replace the embosser system. Although data is not currently available, this replacement system seems to increase workflow, safety and caregiver satisfaction while lowering frustration and costs.

Survey Question to Registration Personnel: Has removal of the Embosser and implementing printed labels made your job easier?

	1= Strongly Disagree	2= Disagree	3= No Change	4= Agree	5= Strongly Agree
Rating	1	2	3	4	5
Responses	0	0	1	3	8
Percentage	0%	0%	8%	25%	67%

De Niles Team—This team tackled lost charges and revenue due to denials. Lost revenue included denials not being appealed, appeals being made too late or being appealed improperly. The team looked for ways to reduce denials, increase the percentage of denials that were appealed and increase the favorable rulings on appeals made. In addition, the team looked at pursuing sources of payment that were available to the hospital but had not been previously pursued. The result:

Medical Necessity Denial by Payer

	Jan 1– Dec 31 2004	Jan 1– Dec 31 2005	Increase $$ Appealed	Reimburse %	Estimated Net $$ 2005
Ambulance	$65,366	$339,446	$274,080	57%	$156,225
All others	$595,341	$992,988	$397,647	28%	$111,341
Unfavorable ambulance appeal to be billed to patient	$0	$43,052	$43,052	50% (est.)	$21,526
Upfront Collections: January 05–June 05 = $42,876					
Upfront Collections: July 05–December 05 = $89,526					

(continued)

Net Increase Upfront Collections: Jul–Dec 05 = $46,650	$46,650	(6 mos.)
Estimated *annual* increased net revenues =	$93,300	$93,300 (ann. est.)
Total Net Benefits Denials by Payer		**$335,742**

Caregiver Satisfaction in Registration on a scale of 1 to 5 (with 1 lowest and 5 highest)

Year	Caregiver Job Satisfaction Average Score
March 2005	3.33
March 2006	4.00

Work-Flow Efficiency Scores from caregivers in Registration on a scale of 1 to 5 with 1 being the lowest and 5 being the highest. Rate the improvement in the following areas over the last year (March 2005 to March 2006):

	Average Score
Workflow created by replacement of the embosser system	4.70
Workflow created by upgrades in computers and equipment	3.80
Workflow creted by the addition of medical abbreviations and dictionaries	3.33
Workflow created by online access to insurance companies	4.40
Improved relationship between Registration and the Business Office	3.70
Overall workflow	4.00

Rehabilitation Center Scheduling Team—This team looked to expand the revenues and community outreach of the Rehabilitation and Wellness Center.

It was determined that the legacy scheduling system at the Center was inefficient, illogical and prone to cause mistakes and frustration among both caregivers and patients. The team recreated the old system, including specifying a computerized system that will replace the old manual system. The results through November 2005 are as follows:

Increase of 30 visits per month (10% increase in productivity) x $150/visit (current billing rate) creates an annual increase in billable revenue of:	$54,000
The new computerized scheduling system is scheduled to go live in August 2006. The expected result of upgrading to the cmputerized scheduling system will be to realize an additional 40–45 visits per month increasing billable annual revenue by:	$81,000

Flo's Fanatics (Nursing) Team—This team was created to look at ways to make the jobs of nurses on the floor easier, more efficient, and more rewarding, while providing higher levels of quality care for patients. It was determined that the clinical staff spent a great deal of time doing things other than serving patients, which adversely affected both caregivers and patients. The following actions were or are being taken:

Data was collected that indicated that clinical caregivers were spending more than 25 percent of their time "hunting and gathering." The team began to address the root causes of this unproductive use of nursing time.

Problem: IV Pumps and Regulators —IV pumps and regulators were found to have a number of problems which included wrong type, broken, missing, stored in a place that took an average of more than five minutes of caregiver's time to locate and secure.

Action: The actual needs of the floor for IV pumps and regulators were determined and the optimum number and types of IV pumps were purchased for all areas of need. All IV pumps were marked with different colored permanent labels to insure that they remained in the proper area. They are now inventoried on a daily basis to insure that each room has the appropriate and necessary IV pumps and regulators available for patients.

Estimated Annual Savings: $39,624 per Year

Problem: Wheelchair Availability—It was discovered that a significant amount of caregivers' time was spent looking for wheelchairs. When wheelchairs were found, many were in disrepair (broken or missing footrests, torn fabric and missing oxygen holders). In addition, wheelchairs were being stolen.

Action: A complete inventory of wheelchairs and the specific condition of each wheelchair was compiled. The optimum number of functional wheelchairs was determined and new ones were purchased where necessary. One specification of the new wheelchairs was a tall bar on the back to prevent theft. All wheelchairs were clearly marked with their proper area. An appropriate oxygen holder has been identified and is being ordered for each wheelchair. Although hard data is not currently available, it appears that having a working wheelchair available when needed saves a great deal of time and frustration among caregivers and patients who need a wheelchair.

Estimated Annual Savings: $35,662 per Year

Problem: The triage form was lengthy and included a significant amount of information that, because of safety and regulatory issues, should have been collected in the main Emergency Department (ED), not in triage. Some nurses were not asking necessary questions when the patient came into the ED, because the questions had already been asked in triage. It is standard and critical policy that nurses in the main ED ask every patient these questions. In cases where nurses are asking questions that have already been asked in triage, there was needless duplication.

Action: Create and implement a new triage form that asks only for the information that is required to get the patient into the ED. Then, the nurses in the ED ask the questions required to assess the patient and provide the best possible clinical care.

Estimated Annual Savings: $24,430 per Year

Improvements Not Yet Quantified (Flo's Fanatics):

Problem: Patients can't always wash their hands when they feel a need to do so.

Action: Supply a personal hospitality package for each patient that includes towelettes, personal grooming, hygiene and other items to make the patient's stay at the hospital more comfortable.

Problem: Tub Room was being used as a makeshift storage room.

Action: Clean out tub room and prepare the room to again be used as a Tub Room, a significant benefit for some patients.

Problem: Some things were not being completed in the discharge process.

Action: A Discharge Checklist was created and implemented in the discharge process.

Problem: Refrigerator in the ER was on the floor and it was difficult (hard on the back) for caregivers to locate meds while bending or squatting.

Action: Raised the Refrigerator to a more optimal level.

Problem: No place for patients to put trash.

Action: A small disposable trash bag was attached to every bed in a place that is convenient for the patient.

Problem: Charts in Chemo taking up significant space to the point where people have difficulty moving around in Chemo.

Action: Move charts to Medical Records into a special section designated for Chemo.

Problem: Too many keys in MedSurg and the ER. Caregivers spent up to five minutes locating the correct key to open various locked areas.

Action: Change locks so that the same key can open more than one lock. Code the keys and locks so that the correct key is easily identified for a particular lock. Currently there are only six (6) keys required to open all the locks that previously required up to 30 keys.

Problem: Supplies on carts for nurses are not optimized to include supplies that are most used by nurses.

Action: Assess carts for usage of specific supplies and optimize inventory levels to restock system based upon usage.

Problem: Some clinical caregivers are having a difficult time working with other caregivers, including Directors.

Action: Chief Nursing Officer (CNO) and Directors to address these issues head-on and in real-time. Improper behavior among caregivers will no longer be tolerated and disciplinary action will be taken against repeat offenders. Identify and contract to bring conflict management training to clinical caregivers at GRMC.

Problem: In MedSurg, caregivers tend to make their first rounds together. This means that it can be as long as one hour that a patient is in a room before seeing a nurse.

Action: Nurses will make rounds separately so that they can get to all the patients in a timely manner.

Problem: There was a lack of direction on the floor when a Director was not present.

Action: A Charge Nurse Program was created and a number of caregivers have become Charge Nurses.

Problem: Pagers are broken or not available for family members waiting for patients.

Action: An inventory of all pagers at GRMC was taken and it was found that all 18 pagers were in disrepair with the majority held together with rubber bands or tape. An assessment of various departments' need for pagers is being initiated, along with an investigation into the most appropriate pager going forward. New pagers have been specified and purchased to replace the old ones.

Recruiting and Retention

CNO Cathy Woodard and David Dibble created a strategy to improve relations with Western New Mexico University (WNMU) in Silver City. A part of this strategy included attracting a higher percentage of graduate nurses to Gila Regional. With costs to recruit and retain nurses being estimated at $50,000 ($10,000 recruiting + $40,000 retention benefit), a significant financial benefit would accrue to Gila Regional if a higher percentage of graduate nurses could be recruited and retained at Gila Regional.

In years past GRMC has been only marginally successful in recruiting graduate nurses from local WNMU. The challenge has only grown with larger hospitals able to pay large sign-on bonuses and offer other benefits that GRMC cannot match. However, Cathy Woodard's efforts dramatically improved the recruiting success of graduate nurses from WNMU to GRMC. Note: Actual data is only available for 2006 with all other years being estimates.

Year	# of Graduate Nurses in the Graduating Class (approx.)	# of Nurses Hired by GRMC	% of Class Hired by GRMC	# Retained by GRMC
2001	20 (est.)	7	35%	6
2002	20 (est.)	3	15%	1
2003	20 (est.)	6	30%	2
2004	25 (est.)	10	40%	8
2005	25 (est.)	10	40%	6
2006	23	18	78%	Data pending 7/07

Based upon average past performance, it is expected that GRMC would attract nine (9) out of the 23 graduate nurses. In fact, GRMC attracted 18 (a gain of nine nurses). Based upon an average hard cost of recruiting a nurse of $10,000 and retention benefits of an additional $40,000 per nurse, the benefits that accrued to GRMC from Cathy and her team's work follow:

Recruiting and Retention Benefits to GRMC		
Hard Cost of Recruiting a Nurse	$10,000 x 9 Additional Nurses	$90,000
Soft Cost of Recruiting and Retaining a Nurse Average Retention 2001–2005 = 63% x $360,000	$40,000 x 9 Additional Nurses = $360,000 x 63% retention 2001–2005	$226,800
Total Benefits to GRMC in Recruiting & Retention of WNMU Graduate Nurses		$316,800

Facilitator Training—David Dibble conducted a five-part facilitator training class for 18 caregivers at GRMC.

Up Up and Away Team—It was decided that GRMC needed more exposure in the outside world as part of a strategy to improve recruiting to the hospital and Silver City. Several Directors decided to write an article about the vision and commitment of GRMC to the New Agreements/Four Agreements and Planetree, including progress that had been made to date. The article was published in a widely read healthcare periodical, *ADVANCE Newsmagazine*. A second article will be published in *ADVANCE Newsmagazine* later this year. Results from the publication of this article are not currently known and additional articles are planned.

Patient Satisfaction is directly related to Caregiver Satisfaction, with a variable lag period. This principle is observable in the remarkable Patient Satisfaction scores achieved by Chemotherapy. It is interesting to note that the big jump in Patient Satisfaction in Chemotherapy occurred almost two years after the introduction of the Four Agreements and later the New Agreements in Chemotherapy. Here we see the connection and lag period between caregiver satisfaction and patient satisfaction.

Chemotherapy: Mike Torres, Director of the Chemotherapy Departent, was the first to begin using the Four Agreements as principles by which his department would operate. Later, he became an early champion for The New Agreements and has been a strong supporter of Planetree. Guided by Mike's leadership, the Chemotherapy staff has created a department that operates within the context of the New Agreements, the Four Agreements and Planetree Patient-Centered Care. In Chemotherapy, the caregivers love Mike, love their jobs, love their patients and love each other in spite of working long hours in a cramped, understaffed, high-stress environment.

The Result: For the quarter ending December 31, 2005, Press-Ganey reports that the Chemotherapy Department at GRMC has achieved the highest patient satisfaction score (96.3) for Chemotherapy Departments of the 24 hospitals surveyed. This score also reflected a significant improvement from past rankings at GRMC.

Press-Gainy Chemotherapy Patient Satisfaction Ranking Compared with Other Hospitals Surveyed							
Q1-04	Q2-04	Q3-04	Q4-04	Q1-05	Q2-05	Q3-05	Q4-05
35	22	40	30	47	55	52	96

Productivity of Meetings at GRMC

It was acknowledged at the beginning of 2005 that meetings in general at GRMC were often only marginally productive. A survey of caregivers (those involved in meetings at GRMC both prior to and after the introduction of New Agreements "Systems-Based" meeting protocol) was conducted to measure change in meeting productivity. The survey was sent to caregivers who have worked on systems improvement teams using the New Agreements Systems-Improvement process. Of the 37 people who received the survey, 26 responded. The results follow:

Question: Using Post-It™ Notes, Putting it on the Wall and Action Items (New Agreements Systems Improvement Tools), do you believe our improvement teams are more productive and successful compared to one year ago?

	1= Much Worse	2= Worse	3= No Change	4= Better	5= Much Better
Score	1	2	3	4	5
Responses	0	0	1	7	18
Percentage	0%	0%	4%	27%	69%

Average Rating 26 Responses: 4.65

Public financial reports indicate that Gila Regional incurred a loss in its fiscal year ending June 30, 2005. Leadership budgeted/projected a profit of $1.8 million for the fiscal year ending June 30, 2006. Actual bottom line profit for 2006 was approximately $2.7 million, an increase over projections of $900,000 (or 150 percent of projected profits).

It appears that an unknown but significant portion of the increased profitability of Gila Regional is the result of New Agreements Healthcare systems-improvement efforts. This type of increase to the bottom line may be essential to the survival of many of America's healthcare organizations.

The key to this type of financial improvement is in focusing on the systems within the organization that create less than preferred financial performance. Whatever the financial performance of any organization (good or not-so-good), it is primarily a function of the systems in which people work. If a leader wants to improve financial performance, she must focus her people's efforts on improving the systems.

Simple. But *only* if the leader is a systems thinker. Otherwise, the systems will be invisible to the leader and she may continue to do things that have little effect on financial performance (i.e., More-Better-Different approaches).

Now that we have looked into how to increase profitability in healthcare, we will move to the next step and explore how you can bring New Agreements Healthcare to your organization and your life. Chapter 7 is about making this body of knowledge real for you and your people.

BRINGING NEW AGREEMENTS HEALTHCARE TO YOUR ORGANIZATION

The end of all education should surely be service to others.
We cannot seek achievement for ourselves and forget about
the progress and prosperity of our community. Our ambitions
must be broad enough to include the aspirations and needs
of others for their sake and for our own.

—Cesar Chavez

I AM NOT SURE WHY I HAVE BECOME A MESSENGER FOR NEW Agreements Healthcare. In all humility, I do not feel the powerful bodies of knowledge that comprise New Agreements Healthcare are mine. Yes, I did format these principles so that they would be accepted and useful to healthcare organizations. And I've learned how to teach the principles in order to make them real for those who want to become teachers and consultants for these bodies of knowledge. However, I'm clear that I am not the source of this remarkable information. I'm sure that no human being is the source of universal principles.

The true source of universal principles is *the* Source, God, Spirit, Higher Consciousness, the Creator, or whatever you choose to call the One who created the universe and its principles, both physical and nonphysical.

I have a vision that New Agreements Healthcare can become a recognized strategy for transforming healthcare in America. For this vision to gain traction, many kindred spirits must be able to teach these bodies of knowledge in healthcare. This is the reason why we have created the New Agreements Healthcare Teacher Training that not only provides tools and techniques for transforming healthcare, but also an experience of the principles which are the foundation of this work. In order to teach this work one must live it to the best of his or her ability. These principles must become "who we are" and how we operate in the world.

It is not enough to talk about the need to care about others. We must *care* about others. It is not enough to talk about the importance of systems thinking. We must *become* systems thinkers. It is not enough to talk about the importance of having a life purpose. We must *be* on purpose. It is not enough to talk about the importance of having a daily practice. We must "practice a little every day." *We must become what we teach.* In this process of *becoming,* Teacher Training students experience gifts in themselves that they may not have known. For others, the training may help them regain a part of themselves that had been lost along the way in life's journey.

This is an appeal to the healthcare leaders at all levels in their organizations to learn and practice this work in some way. The Teacher Training is so integral to realizing the vision that its function must be explained, understood, promoted, and ultimately become part of any New Agreements Healthcare implementation.

While implementing New Agreements Healthcare in healthcare organizations will require outside support in the beginning, without internal teachers and champions, the speed and sustainability of the desired changes may be jeopardized. The Teacher Training creates internal and external leaders, teachers and consultants for the work. However, it is the internal leaders, teachers and consultants who maintain momentum and insure stability while implementing New Agreements Healthcare. These skilled human resources are *essential* to the long-term success and sustainability of New Agreements Healthcare.

The Teacher Training is comprised of five full days on-site, two teleconference classes over approximately two months and an additional five full days on-site. An optional Mentors/Teachers Program (where graduates of the Teacher Training return to support and teach in the Teacher Training) is offered. This advanced training is highly recommended for those who want to go deeper into the work. As we teach what we need to learn, so we learn the most when we teach.

The Teacher Training is a life-changing experience. Most of all, it works. This training creates an experience of the material that's being taught. Since it is experiential, the training accelerates the learning curve for students, making the principles easy to teach and apply in the workplace in a short period of time. Students *become* teachers.

The Evolution of Student to New Agreements Teacher

I HAD ONE OF THE MOST INSPIRING DAYS OF MY WORKING LIFE IN JULY 2006. Linda and I watched one of our students in the New Agreements Healthcare Teacher Training *become* the message he wanted to take into the world and the workplace. Brian is the Director of the Rehab Center at Gila Regional Medical Center. When we started doing this work in the Rehab Center, it was like working in a hornet's nest of gossip, unhappiness and dysfunctional systems. Here's what Brian had to say a year ago.

> "I wasn't sure what more I could do. Long hours and stress were taking their toll. I was concerned that my health was starting to be effected. I've always been a dedicated employee but in these last few years, I've been plagued by the realization that something important is missing in my work life. There is just so much firefighting and drama. And resistance to change. It's draining."

Here's what Brian says now.

> "Today those with poor attitudes have left the organization. This created space for enthusiastic, talented, kindred spirits to show up who are excited to change, grow, and do this work. It has also renewed the spirit and energy of those people who have been with the Center for years, but were frustrated by the negative people and poor systems."

Brian invited his team to work with him on a major problem that, if it could not be solved, had the power to bring the Rehab Center to its knees. The problem was that Medicare unilaterally made the decision to no longer pay for technicians who do as much as 50 percent of the work at the Center. Going forward, Medicare would only pay for Physical Therapists (PTs).

Medicare comprises 50 percent of the Center revenue. Brian brought his whole team together and began using the New Agreements Systems Tools to look at the current systems and identify where changes could be made to mitigate the problem. The whole group was animated and engaged. Ideas flew in from every direction. Brian facilitated the whole thing.

In two short hours, new systems were co-created by the people and an implementation strategy and follow-up actions were completed. Watching Brian, I felt like I was watching myself in front of the room.

Linda said the same thing. "David, I thought I was watching you up there. Brian was absolutely masterful." I had tears in my eyes watching the student become the teacher.

With the new system in place, the Gila Regional Rehabilitation Center will not be adversely affected by the changes in Medicare. They have not had to lay off or fire anyone.

Conversely, another Rehab Center in the region, which also faced this same problem, elected to fire all their Techs and only use PTs for Rehab. This Center has now shut down due to the fact that a PT-only Rehab Center is not a viable business model (it loses lots of money).

As you see, the New Agreements Teacher Training is an accelerated learning modality that creates leaders and teachers who can sustain and advance this much-needed knowledge in the real-world of healthcare.

At the conclusion of the Teacher Training, Brian Cunningham said this:

"The New Agreements Teacher Training has helped me to ground this work in measurable action. I am now able to consistently apply this work at all levels of the job. As a result of this work, I am becoming a real leader in the sense that I am now training others in my department how to be leaders."

What makes the Teacher Training so powerful is a combination of cutting edge curriculum and the way the Program is taught using a "pull" strategy. Although there are many opportunities to challenge yourself and grow professionally and personally, it's important to note that no one is ever pushed. It's the same way for how New Agreements Healthcare is taught in organizations. Powerful, yet gentle.

The curriculum itself is cutting edge while at the same time tapping into ancient wisdom. The bodies of knowledge that are taught in the Teacher Training include, but are not limited to, the following:

- The New Agreements in Healthcare
- The Four Agreements
- The Masteries
- Systems Thinking
- New Agreements Systems-Improvement Tools and Techniques
- New Agreements DreamWork from *DreamWork: Dream Interpretation* (life purpose and vision work)
- New Agreements CharacterTypes from *DreamWork: CharacterTypes* (leadership and management based on how people think, communicate and relate)

Any one of these bodies of knowledge could be the work of a lifetime. Together they are a roadmap for healing healthcare, changing lives at work and home, and transforming our world. Experiences that accelerate learning in the Teacher Training include the following:

- Daily practices such as yogic breathing, chanting and meditation
- High Ropes Course
- Native American Sweat Lodge
- African Drumming
- Many additional in-class group- and team-learning exercises and simulations

Here's what graduates say about New Agreements Healthcare Teacher Training.

"The New Agreements Teacher Training has given me new insights into myself and my work. The New Agreements creates a framework for a holistic approach to the operations of an organization. We all know intuitively that it is a combination of the people and the systems that effect how well an organization operates. The New Agreements embrace the development of the people while setting them up to be successful through optimization of the systems in which they must work. This training is a model for success in healthcare."
—Sue Nieboer, RN, MPA
VP Operations, Gerber Memorial Health Systems

"The New Agreements Teacher Training has been an incredible growth experience. I've learned to lead in a whole new way. The

Teacher Training has gifted me with immediately useful systems tools, management and leadership education, accountability, and love."
—Cathy Woodward
Chief Nursing Officer, Gila Regional Medical Center

"Participating in New Agreements Healthcare Teacher Training has been a terrific way to incorporate the critical elements of personal growth, caring for staff, and systems work into a successful method for transforming healthcare. It is very clear that improving the work environment with a focus on people and the equal emphasis on solving systems challenges will improve patient care and patient safety."
—Rick van Pelt, M.D.

"The Teacher Training has been a life expanding experience in the areas of leadership, team building and systems thinking. It's one thing to know as leaders that we should love, grow and serve our people but quite another to really feel it. Combining that with learning to fix the legacy systems that have hampered my people for years is a success strategy that is workable in any organization. Results created at GRMC using the tools learned in this program include higher employee satisfaction and improved performance."
—John Madrid, MHA
Director of Imaging Services, Gila Regional Medical Center

"The New Agreements Teacher Training has moved me to recognized patterns in my personal and work life that have kept me from being my best. By learning the disciplines of the New

Agreements, I am now clear about my life's purpose, which is to love and inspire others to use their gifts and talents in a way that brings joy and success to the workplace. I have new tools to address the need for change in the healthcare system that includes staff at all levels of the organization. This results in happy, productive workers and rapid change in systems and processes. I feel I'm now prepared to live my life purpose and make a real difference in the world."
—Jan Stone, MS, RN
Clinical Director, Gerber Memorial Health Systems

"The tools that I learned in the New Agreements Teacher Training have enabled me to grow as a person and a leader. Having David as a resource while initiating these tools and techniques has helped to accelerate the successful implementation of both the New Agreements and the Four Agreements in our hospital."
—Mindy Suhr, RN, MBA/HCM
Director of Maternal Child Health

"This program met all my expectations and beyond. I was able to open my heart to discover and learn about my true self and what makes me tick. This in turn I apply to my work and family. The learning experiences are diverse and I loved the group learning. I was able to walk away and apply the systems improvement tools immediately. Importantly, I have discovered the courage to continue on my path of personal and professional growth while learning how to enjoy life and work at a whole new level."
—Ann Jordan, RN, OT
Manager of Rehabilitation Therapies, Scripps Healthcare

I encourage anyone who feels pulled to this work in some way to speak personally with these Teacher Training Graduates. It is one thing to see what people have written but it's even more powerful to talk to people and feel their enthusiasm from the experience.

At GRMC we learned valuable lessons along the way, which we are taking with us to both the Teacher Training and future New Agreements Healthcare assignments at other healthcare organizations. In the next chapter, lessons learned push themselves to the front of the class.

LESSONS LEARNED

Only two kinds of people can attain self-knowledge ... those whose
minds are not overcrowded with thoughts borrowed from others;
and those who, after studying all the scriptures and sciences,
have come to realize that they know nothing.

—Ramakrishna Paramahamsadeva

WITH ANY MEANINGFUL VENTURE, NOT EVERYTHING WILL PROCEED as predicted. The organizational change work we did at Gila Regional was meaningful. In some cases, it was clearly cutting edge. We made mistakes, had many learning experiences and initiated many course corrections along the way. As we talked about in the New Agreements Systems Tools section of this book, we can assume that 20 percent of the learning incidents contributed 80 percent of the impact on the Program. This 80/20 split seems born out in the lessons learned category, too. Here are things that jumped up to bite us and that should be considered thoughtfully before embarking on a real program of change in healthcare.

*My pizza parlor is more thoroughly computerized
than most of healthcare.*

—Don Berwick MD, President, CEO, and cofounder of the Institute for
Healthcare Improvement

Information Technology (IT)

THE IT SYSTEMS AT GRMC BADLY NEEDED TO BE UPGRADED AS WELL AS the skill sets of people who were responsible for IT. This is not a knock of GRMC or the people in IT. This is true for most hospitals in America. If we are upgrading systems in healthcare, we are going to run full-bore into IT very early in the game. I believe it is important to keep in mind that almost all long-term, meaningful systems upgrades are going to be connected to IT. It is the basic nature of the healthcare business that it requires more IT integration and solutions in order to survive and prosper.

It should be noted that GRMC has now attracted talented IT leadership and is in the process of creating a solid IT infrastructure from which to build and upgrade its IT capabilities. It appears that all healthcare organizations should strongly look at IT as a strategic imperative for future growth, cost containment, quality measures, patient and caregiver satisfaction as well as systems upgrades.

Data Mining

IN CONJUNCTION WITH POOR IT SYSTEMS CAME THE INABILITY TO EASILY extract data from the system. Data is gold when doing this type of work. For the most part, it became even more precious as most of this "gold" had to be extracted by hand. Even the most basic tools for gathering and manipulating data were virtually nonexistent. It was only through determined efforts of caregivers at Gila Regional that we were able to collect important data and measurements from the system.

Resistance to Change

WE KNOW THAT CHANGE CAN BE CHALLENGING FOR ORGANIZATIONS AND people. Still, I was surprised at times by how virulent the resistance was among a small group of caregivers at GRMC. These were most-ly employees who had been with the hospital for many years. In some cases, the more good we did and the more measurable the improvements, the more resistance we experienced. If you and your organization are going to change and grow, *really change and grow*, expect resistance.

The more you change and grow, the more shrill will be the wails of those committed to maintaining the status quo. The good news is, little by little, the resistance will dissipate as more caregivers experi-ence the good this change will bring (both professionally and person-ally) in their relationships with patients and co-workers.

Leadership

WITHOUT STRONG LEADERSHIP, THERE IS VIRTUALLY ZERO POSSIBILITY OF making the kind of changes we made at GRMC. It starts at the top. CEO John Rossfeld had to be at the top of his game to balance the day-to-day operations of the hospital while providing time, resources and support for the systems-improvement teams.

He maintained his vision for the hospital and the community. He fielded complaints from Nay-Sayers who urged him to "go back to the way things used to be." John was tested. However, he never wavered. Only with strong leadership at the top can these necessary changes in healthcare be made real.

In addition to strong leadership at the top, able leadership must emerge throughout the organization. This type of widely dispersed leadership is what makes meaningful change sustainable. This is what happened at GRMC.

Some of the strongest, most committed leadership at GRMC now resides in the Chief Nursing Officer (CNO), Chief Medical Officer (CMO), Chief Information Officer (CIO) and the Directors responsible for the Wellness Center, Medical Imaging, Chemotheropy, Planetree, Maternal Child Health, the Emergency Room, Med/Surg, the Business Office, Registration, Marketing and more. At these levels of leadership, New Agreements Healthcare and Planetree programs are becoming part of the hospital culture. More and more, it is the way we do business. It is *who we are*.

Rate of Change and Support for Change

BECAUSE GILA REGIONAL WAS THE FIRST HOSPITAL TO ATTEMPT TO implement New Agreements Healthcare, we had a significant vested interest in the hospital being successful. In other words, whatever we could contribute to insure success for the hospital was provided.

It appears that in the formative stages of the implementation (the first 12 to 18 months) a twice monthly consultation visit was necessary. Following the formative stage, it appears that a once monthly consultation visit (for a period of 6 to 12 months) is an optimum level of support. This indicates that sustainable change at a 50-bed hospital with 650 caregivers (such as Gila Regional) can be realized in 18 to 30 months. This rate of organizational transformation far exceeds the expected rate for a hospital of this size (which, if successful, would normally require five to seven years).

Teaching Teachers and the Need for Skilled Internal Champions

IN THE JUST-CONCLUDED NEW AGREEMENTS HEALTHCARE TEACHER TRAINING, a team of five caregivers from Gila Regional (including the CNO, CMO, and Directors of Wellness, Imaging, and Maternal Child Care) graduated.

Over the term of the Teacher Training, these caregivers became stronger and more skilled at implementing and sustaining systems and cultural changes at the hospital. This group bonded at deeper levels with higher levels of commitment and virtually no fear of the challenges that will surely emerge as the change initiative continues to unfold at the hospital. They enjoy and support each other at work and outside of work.

These incredible people have become teachers in their own right because the Teacher Training creates a new kind of leader and manager who can carry this work forward on their own and sustain momentum. These people have become the glue which will move the implementation forward long after we are gone. The Teacher Training works and is a vital key to creating momentum and sustainability of New Agreements Healthcare at Gila Regional.

The above lessons represent our most comprehensive learning experiences to date. We are assured that many more opportunities to learn and grow will present themselves as we take this work forward. This is a natural part of the great possibility of birthing a new vision for healthcare in America.

In Chapter 9, we test the limits of our vision for the future. What is it that we are to become? What is our role in the coming transformation of healthcare in America? We are looking at nothing less than "Getting Well: The Body-Mind-Spirit Connection."

GETTING WELL:
THE BODY-MIND-SPIRIT
CONNECTION

A Short History of Medicine

2000 B.C. – Here, eat this root.
1000 B.C. – That root is heathen, say this prayer.
1850 A.D. – That prayer is superstition, drink this potion.
1940 A.D. – That potion is snake oil, swallow this pill.
1985 A.D. – That pill is ineffective, take this antibiotic.
2000 A.D. – That antibiotic is artificial. Here, eat this root.

—Author Unknown

THE GREATEST HEALING FORCE AND ONE THAT'S MOST EASY TO APPLY is *love*. In nearly every instance, where an unexpected healing or a miraculous recovery has taken place, we find caring, compassion or some other manifestations of love is a critical contributor. A part of each one of us—each human being—knows the healing-power of love.

Death of a Fisherman

PRIOR TO THE CALL IN 1984, WE HAD HAD A LOT OF CANCER IN OUR FAMILY. My grandmother and my aunt had died from the disease when I was a boy and my little sister, Lorie, died of lymphoma when she was only 34. Although I loved my grandmother and my aunt and felt their losses greatly, the loss of Lorie was devastating. Lorie was tall, beautiful, athletic, creative, loving and the funniest woman I have ever known. She and I could get each other laughing so hard that she would fight to avoid "pee pants" and I would beg for mercy. Her agonizing death greatly affected our whole family.

On a crisp winter day in 1984, I got the call from Dad. He informed me that he had been diagnosed with lung cancer and was scheduled for immediate surgery to remove the diseased lung. After surgery, he would have aggressive chemotherapy and radiation treatments. I asked if I could visit and he said he preferred that I wait until after the treatments—that he did not expect to be good company. The wait turned out to be ten months.

The treatments bordered on intolerable. My dad liked his doctors and knew they were doing their best to arrest the cancer. Still, he also told me after his last chemo treatment that it would be his last even if it meant dying.

"Better dead than to be that sick, son," he lamented.

In the fall of 1985, Dad called to tell me that he was going home from the hospital after his checkup with his oncologist. The checkup had not gone well. The cancer had spread and there was nothing more the doctors could do. He was told to go home and "enjoy the last three or four months of your life."

I was angry. I thought, *After all he had endured. That's it? Go home and "enjoy the last three of four months of your life?"* It just wasn't fair. There had to be something we could do. I put my anger to work.

Call to Action

I DETERMINED TO READ EVERYTHING I COULD LAY MY HANDS ON THAT offered alternative methods of treating cancer. I read about diet, exercise, laughter, meditation, contemplation, visualizations and more. I sifted through tales of miracle machines, energy healings, rain forest plants and herbs, and clinics that were healing cancer in foreign countries after having been driven out of the US by the FDA. What was true and what was hoax?

Still, some of this resonated within me. I determined that Dad did not have to die if he was willing to change his life, *really* change his life. When I had gathered all the information possible in this mad dash against time, I called Dad and asked if I could visit him and talk about what I had learned about alternative methods of treating cancer. He was both curious and happy that I was coming to visit him.

When I arrived at his front door, Dad greeted me like never before. Although his once rock-hard body was now weak and frail, he hugged me strongly and for a long time. Was this really my dad, the one who never touched or opened up? It was. Yet, something in him had changed.

I told Dad that I did not think he had to die, if he chose to live. However, the only way he was going to get better was if he was willing to change—big time. I shared all of the information I had collected and asked if he was willing to commit to any of the method-ologies. He seemed hopeful and I even saw little flashes of enthusi-asm. After some careful thought, he chose to try changes in diet, a strict (if limited) exercise program, visualization and possibly med-itation. He would also quit smoking, which had been an on-again, off-again proposition, even after the discovery of his cancer. As addi-tional support, I committed to go on the macrobiotic diet with him.

As a part of his healing, we agreed that as soon as he was strong enough (well enough), we would fulfill one of his lifelong dreams. We would travel together to Costa Rica, the one place that he had always dreamed of seeing before his death. The third member of our traveling team would be Jim, one of my best friends and one of Dad's favorite people.

Then, I handed my father a present that I saved in case we reached this magic moment. He opened the gift the way a young boy opens Santa's best present under the Christmas tree. Inside the heavy box were books, brochures and travel information on Costa Rica. I told him that since he had been the navigator in the war and on the tuna boats, he would be our navigator, too. He should start planning our itinerary.

Miracles as Usual

FROM THE FIRST DAY OF MY VISIT, DAD BEGAN TO IMPROVE. HE CHANGED his life. He was consistent in his wellness practices. He called often to tell me about his little victories or ideas for our Costa Rica journey. Sometimes his energy was so vibrant that I began to ques-tion my own aliveness. Six months into his wellness practice, he said something that both chilled and delighted me, "David, the cancer is gone."

"How do you know that?" I asked with care, so as not to dampen the moment.

"David, I just know." And he did.

Back at the hospital the doctors were dumbfounded. Dad was supposed to be dead, very dead. Instead, he was not only alive, but also well. He was cancer-free. He became a medical marvel for which the doctors had no explanation. Their enthusiastic advice now became, "We don't know what you're doing, but whatever it is, keep doing it!"

Ten Days in Costa Rica

IN NOVEMBER 1986, JIM, DAD AND I RENTED A SMALL VAN AT THE AIRPORT in San Jose, the capitol of Costa Rica.

Luckily, the old fisherman hadn't lost his navigational touch, so we had full confidence in his ability to guide us to the best sights. Besides, based upon all the books and notes he brought with him, we were sure he had studied everything ever written about Costa Rica. Our only caveat was that we would be always in the moment and allow the trip to unfold. We would be like the wind, free to follow the path of least resistance, free to change in an instant, free to be inspired and joyful during each moment of this most magical journey.

The ten days we spent together in Costa Rica were, without a doubt, the most satisfying and gratifying of my life with Dad. He was open, funny, emotional and gracious. He was alive with gratitude for every sight and sound—and for the company, too. I saw the little kid

GETTING WELL: THE BODY-MIND-SPIRIT CONNECTION

in my dad, the parts of every father that are usually hidden from their sons in the name of adulthood and parenting. Even today, I can still hear the laughter over beer and tacos. Jim, Dad and I jostled to "one-up" the other with the most outrageous story, swearing absolute truth all the while. I also heard stories of life that I had never heard before, stories of my dad's life. After Costa Rica, my Dad and I became even closer—good friends.

The Continuing Saga of Life

TWO YEARS AFTER COSTA RICA, DAD LOST HIS JOB AT THE SHIPYARD WHERE he was a welder. The company had to restructure in order to become more competitive and the older workers were the first to go. No age discrimination, of course. Just coincidence. The law required that he have a chest X-ray before being laid off. He was given a clean bill of health and told to stay in touch, that more work, like prosperity, was just around the corner. Dad checked every day, but the work never came. Unfortunately, the work must have taken a wrong turn and headed out of the country where wages were lower and profits higher.

Dad looked everywhere for work. First he looked for another welding position. Later, he applied for anything. Anything! But, as Dad pointed out, "Seems like they don't want us old fellas. No luck today, but tomorrow's a new day." Brave words, but no job.

Dad had always been a hard worker. He took pride in his work. He needed to work. But, as endless rejections bowed his once strong shoulders, his energy and will sagged. After a while, I think he just gave up.

Three months after the lay-off, my Dad stopped exercising and began smoking again. The diet went by the wayside, too. He mentioned that he wasn't feeling himself and was planning to see the doctor. Four months after the lay-off, the cancer was everywhere.

Dad said, "The bugger is back and I'm too tired to fight it this time."

The Last Father's Day

MY DAD AND MY SISTER JUDY HAD THEIR DIFFERENCES. THEY HADN'T SEEN or spoken to each other in more than five years. I invited Judy to come with me to Texas to visit Dad on Father's Day, reminding her that the cancer was spreading fast and that he probably didn't have much time left. I'd even pay for the trip. Although it was a difficult decision for her, Judy bravely chose to come with me.

I called my Dad a week before Father's Day. As usual, even though he was weak, he perked up when I called. I told him I had a surprise for him. He said that I shouldn't send him anything, that he had everything he needed.

I told him I wasn't sending anything but that I would deliver my gift to him in person. The phone went silent and I knew he was wiping away a tear or two. After a minute, he came back onto the phone and started to tell me how much my coming meant to him. Then I relayed my other news.

"Dad, I have another part to this surprise. Judy is coming with me." I heard the phone fumbled and then hit the floor as Dad sobbed quietly.

I will never forget the sparkle of pure joy that shone in his blue eyes as we met him at the entrance to the Veteran's Hospital. He moved with a combination of a shuffle and a hop, rather like he was dancing or doing a little jig. Waving all the while, his dance carried that stooped old body to meet his kids. He grabbed and hugged Judy in a way that I had never seen before, tears streaming down his pale, wrinkled, weathered face. He kept repeating the words, "You're so beautiful. You're so beautiful."

He spent the better part of the day shuffling us to meet the nurses, doctors and all the friends he'd made at the hospital. His bragging about us should have been embarrassing. It wasn't. It brought tears over and over to those had come to know my dad in his final days.

Moreover, it brought tears to Judy and me. After all, it was Father's Day, Dad's day, the fisherman's day. Dad wasn't a real religious man, but he told me later that it was an inspiration and a gift from God that we had come to be with him on his last Father's Day.

Dad went downhill fast after Father's Day. The last thing he told me was that the time he spent with Judy and me on his last Father's Day was the happiest day of his life. It was a bit of a miracle that a person could be in such ecstasy in a tired, worn-out, diseased old body like the one that carried around my dad.

A Connection to Wellness and Healing

THE PURPOSE OF THIS STORY IS TO ILLUSTRATE THE POWER OF THE BODY-mind-spirit connection and its correlation to disease, wellness and healing. My dad, in some sort of body-mind-spirit dynamic, created his cancer, then healed himself completely, and then recreated his cancer again.

In many ways, healthcare in America is where my dad was when he was sent home to "enjoy the last three or four months of your life."

In these cases, it appears that everything that can be done has been done. Yet the cancer continues to spread. Every effort has been made. Yet the patient edges ever closer to life support. It's time to look outside the box. We have nothing to lose.

To reverse its decline, healthcare in America appears to be in need of a new mindset, new types of tools and a higher purpose of some sort—a body-mind-spirit connection of it own. New Agreements Healthcare is about the creation of these connections toward healing and a movement toward wellness in healthcare itself.

We need the wonderful skill sets, tools, and technologies that allow physicians and other caregivers to perform "minor miracles" in treating, curing, and healing the sick and injured. This is Western medicine at its best. But there are other tools, techniques and healing methodologies that can also become part of mainstream American healthcare.

Complementary and Alternative Medicine (CAM)

CAM IS ALMOST ALWAYS A MORE HOLISTIC APPROACH TO HEALING THAN traditional Western medicine. This in no way takes away from the contribution Western medicine makes in healing and treating the sick and injured. What it does do is bring into balance more of the body-mind-spirit connection that must be a part of the creation of a new American healthcare system. It is only the entrenched mindsets of the various constituencies that make up the current healthcare system that prevent this blending and balance of both physical and non-physical treatment modalities. We must remember that many CAM therapies have been around for thousands of years. By comparison, it was a "blink of an eye" in the past that mainstream medicine once advocated bleeding sick patients and practiced surgery without anesthesia or antiseptic measures.

This is not to make Western medicine wrong. It is to point out how we get stuck in a mindset and tend to discount anything outside the currently accepted belief system. In the sequence of human evolution (including the evolution of healthcare), the mind is always the last to get it. Which leads us to look at where all this transformation may be taking us.

> *Of the 83 million people in the US, 42 percent of the population make 243 million visits per year to providers of CAM. While not usually covered by health insurance, these visits make up a larger percentage of visits to healthcare providers than visits to traditional primary care physicians (PCP). In addition, 40 percent of people who use CAM do not tell their PCP about the visits for fear of how their PCP will react.*
> —Susan Frampton, Laura Gilpin and Patrick Charmel,
> *Putting Patients First: Designing and Practicing Patient-Centered Care*

Wellness: The Ultimate Healthcare System

WE HAVE EXPLORED THINGS WE CAN DO TO BRIDGE THE GAP BETWEEN our current condition in healthcare and what we ultimately must become. Fixing systems, loving and growing our people, living our higher purpose and balancing traditional Western medicine with CAM are workable ways to enhance the current system, improve quality of care and financial performance, and re-energize our caregivers.

However, this is not our ultimate destination. It is only a bridge to our ultimate destination. Our ultimate destination is a condition called *wellness*. Wellness of the whole—body, mind and spirit.

The body is meant to be well. We can make the case that it is the mind that draws illness, accidents and other misfortune that require ongoing visits to the doctor or drug store to us. Notice that people who do not have a lot of fear bouncing around in their minds don't seem to get sick as often or pull as many accidents to themselves. Look in your own life. When do you get sick? I'll wager it is usually when you have something stressful going on in your life.

An estimated 60 to 90 percent of doctor visits involve stress-related complaints.
—*Newsweek*, September 27, 2004

The Role of Stress in Our Lives

AMERICA IS BECOMING A NATION OF STRESS CASES. THE THINGS WE STRESS about are, for the most part, not real. They are made up by the mind. The mind spins out fearful thoughts, beliefs and memories that keep us in the past and future, where life does not exist. Life is lived only in the moment. Unless you're being chased by a tiger, it's almost impossible to be stressed in the moment where life is lived.

We tend to handle stress by identifying with the mind and doing things to temporarily reduce stress and anxiety. Many times we do things on "automatic pilot." These activities include eating when we are not hungry, drinking when we are not thirsty, or placating ourselves with diversions (such as watching television, buying things we probably don't need, or indulging in other habits that may be hindering our well-being).

Transforming American Healthcare toward Wholeness and Wellness

WE KNOW THAT PATIENT SATISFACTION IS A FUNCTION OF CAREGIVER satisfaction. Wellness in patients may also be a function of wellness in caregivers. Transforming American healthcare will require that caregivers begin moving toward a condition that we might define as wholeness or wellness. This means going beyond the body and our usually unexamined life and beginning to transform the mind, too.

The mind creates an individual's reality. Because we are about to transform the current reality in healthcare, we must begin to model the change we want to see in the world. When you are well, you are in a position to assist others in becoming well. Is this not what caregiving is all about? It is time that we begin to live our higher purpose, which requires evolving to a higher state of mindfulness. If we are to be the change we want to see in healthcare, we must become whole, complete and well. There's no greater adventure than living a purposeful life in service to self and others. With great love and compassion, I ask, until we meet again, *be well.*

EPILOGUE

Native American Wisdom

If we look at the path we do not see the sky.
We are earth people on a journey to the stars.
Our quest, our earth walk is to look within to know who we are,
to see that we are connected to all things,
that there is no separation, only in the mind.

—Author Unknown

IT APPEARS THAT WE ARE COMING UPON A DEFINING MOMENT IN THE evolution of healthcare in America. We are about to experience changes in a system that has become so dysfunctional that it is now feeding upon itself. It is eating the life energy of the caregivers, physicians and patients who work in and depend upon this system for their financial, physical and emotional wellness.

Rather than healing, it has now become a source of its own brand of sickness. The system is driving its best caregivers and physicians out of the profession while the pipeline of new people coming into healthcare continues to shrink. Many of the people who remain in the system do so in tired bodies and burnt-out minds, hoping that it will somehow get better. It won't. It can't. This sick beast cannot be fixed. It must be transformed—*starting now.*

A tidal wave of demographics now races toward American healthcare as the population rapidly becomes older, heavier and sicker. Those with chronic lifestyle diseases, which have no cure within the current healthcare system, will fill our ERs and hospital beds. All this, as tens of millions of baby boomers are now beginning to turn 60.

And what do we get for the highest premium healthcare systems in the industrialized world? Not nearly enough. Quality of healthcare in America continues to decline while costs continue to rise. This is not a scenario that appears will end happily. Or is it?

Sometimes the most dire circumstances provide the greatest opportunity for meaningful change. I believe this is the case for healthcare in America. Change is coming to the healthcare systems whether we want it or not. The question is—will we be proactive or reactive as things begin to shift?

New Agreements Healthcare and the Four Agreements offer a workable roadmap for the transformation of healthcare organizations. We also offer a longer term guide for the ultimate destination of healthcare in America. That destination is called *wellness*. Wellness is more than a body without disease. Wellness is holistic. Wellness includes body, mind and spirit. When we are well, the world becomes a better place.

It is a universal truth that the mind is fearful of anything unlike itself. Because people identify with their minds, they feel fear about change that takes them outside the "box" of the existing mindset.

This is why resistance to change is so natural and predictable. It is also why a high level of fear and apprehension may appear among some as the coming changes in healthcare begin to manifest.

There is nothing to fear. We will be fine. These changes are a natural evolution of systems. As the human elements within the healthcare system, we will change, grow and transform with it.

I encourage those of you who chose to be proactive with the coming changes to muster a little courage. Courage allows us to step through our fears and stepping through fear is the most efficient way to transcend it. On the other side of our fears is the freedom that makes our hearts sing and helps us manifest the life we were meant to live. Maybe even our life's purpose.

At the end of the day, the New Agreements and the Four Agreements go beyond dysfunctional systems, quality of care, costs and the bottom line. The New Agreements and the Four Agreements are really about life. They are about proactively creating the life we are meant to live, both at work and at home. When we live our lives in gratitude, service and love, the people around us heal. And the human condition is raised up a little bit.

To this end, this is what all universal teaching is about. As Gandhi reminded us so well, "Be the change you want to see in the world."

The great R. Buckminster Fuller tells us that there is one thing to do in the human experience: We must *love comprehensively*. To the best of your ability, live the Agreements. Lead with courage, compassion, and respect for all. Change and grow. Be the change you want to see in healthcare, at home and in the world.

And be well.

RESOURCES AND NEXT STEPS

New Agreements Healthcare Teacher Training

Learn to apply and teach New Agreements Healthcare in your health-care organization. The Teacher Training Program consists of ten full days plus two teleconference classes over two to three months. For information and an application, go to www.TheNewAgreements.com or contact David via e-mail at David@TheNewAgreements.com.

Consulting and Training

David believes that transformation of the workplace is the key to transforming our world. David consults with and trains healthcare and other organizations that wish to move to higher levels of con-sciousness, purpose and measurable performance. If you want to bring New Agreements Healthcare into your workplace, contact David via e-mail at David@TheNewAgreements.com.

Keynote Presentations

Bring David to your meeting to share with your group the power of the New Agreements and the Four Agreements in the workplace. David is a dynamic presenter who inspires his audiences with real-world stories from the workplace, belly-laugh humor and abundant audience participation. Contact David to book a whole new presentation experience for your healthcare or business group via e-mail at David@TheNewAgreements.com.

The New Agreements in Healthcare

To purchase additional copies of *The New Agreements in Healthcare: Healing a Healthcare System on Life Support* go to www.TheNewAgreements.com.

Individual Work

Linda Dibble, David's wife of 35 years, has taught the New Agreements, the Four Agreements, CharacterTypes and DreamWork for more than fifteen years. She works with both individuals and groups. To work with Linda one-on-one or in a group, contact her via e-mail at Linda@TheNewAgreements.com.

DreamWork and CharacterTypes Books

Purchase copies of David Dibble's books on the revolutionary bodies of knowledge *DreamWork: Dream Interpretation* and *DreamWork: Character Types*. To order, go to www.TheNewAgreements.com.

The New Agreements in the Workplace

To purchase copies of *The New Agreements in the Workplace: Releasing the Human Spirit* with a foreword by don Miguel Ruiz (author of the worldwide bestseller, *The Four Agreements*), go to www.TheNewAgreements.com, your local bookstore, or www.Amazon.com.

New Agreements Healthcare in Action

For a firsthand account of the experience of bringing New Agreements Healthcare to the world, contact the champions who actually did the work at Gila Regional Medical Center (GRMC):

John Rossfeld – CEO

Jean Remillard, MD – CMO (Teacher Training Graduate)

Cathy Woodward – CNO (Teacher Training Graduate)

Brian Cunningham – Director, Wellness and Rehabilitation Center (Teacher Training Graduate)

Mike Torrez – Director, Chemotherapy

Dan Otero – Director, Planetree

John Madrid – Director, Medical Imaging (Teacher Training Graduate)

Mindy Suhr – Director, Maternal Child Health (Teacher Training Graduate)

Anne Hinton – Director, Business Office

Wanda True – Director, ER

Denise Baird – Director, Med/Surg

Main GRMC Phone Number – 505-538-4000 and Web site address – http://www.grmc.org/

General Contact Information for New Agreements, Inc.

PO Box 2674, Rancho Santa Fe, CA 92067

Telephone David at 760-431-7893

E-mail: David@TheNewAgreements.com

Telephone Linda at 760-431-1136

E-mail: Linda@TheNewAgreements.com

Fax: 760-431-7899

Web site address – www.TheNewAgreements.com